ISAIAH 40-55

CHRISTOPHER R. NORTH

Professor Emeritus of Hebrew
University College of North Wales
Bangor

SCM PRESS LTD
BLOOMSBURY STREET LONDON

To the Memory of my Teacher
CHARLES LEES BEDALE
whose untimely Death in the First World War
was a grievous Loss
to Old Testament Learning

334 00728 3

First published 1952
Second impression 1956
Third impression 1959
Fourth impression 1964
Fifth impression 1966
Sixth impression 1969
Seventh impression 1971
Eighth impression 1974

© *SCM Press Ltd 1956*

Printed in Great Britain by
Fletcher & Son Ltd, Norwich

CONTENTS

INTRODUCTION

COMMENTARY

I

II

VI

VII

VIII

IX

X

XI

XII

XIII

XIV

XV

XVI

PREFACE

The literature on Isaiah 40-55 is enormous. I have, of course, made extensive use of books and articles in languages other than English. In particular, I am indebted to the commentaries of Professor Aage Bentzen (Danish) and the late Professor Paul Volz (German), but limitation of space does not permit detailed references. I have ventured to include in the Bibliography a few of the most important foreign works.

The Commentary is based on the Authorized Version (AV), but readings from the Revised Version (RV) and its margins (marg.) have been frequently quoted. EVV indicates a reading common to both the standard English Versions. DSI denotes a reading from the Dead Sea Scroll of Isaiah belonging to St. Mark's Monastery, Jerusalem. LXX stands for the Septuagint Greek translation. DI is an abbreviation for the Prophet, Deutero-Isaiah.

The Commentary is plentifully sprinkled with brackets and parentheses. This is inevitable in any commentary, especially if the author is restricted to a given number of words. To get everything in, and in the right proportions, is like fitting pieces into a jigsaw puzzle.

My thanks are due to my colleague, Mr. D. R. Ap-Thomas, M.A., B.D., for checking the Scripture references, and to my wife for assisting with the proofs.

C. R. NORTH

Bangor, 1952

PREFACE TO THE SECOND EDITION

This little book was first published in 1952. Since then I have made a further intensive study of the chapters with which it deals. The results of this will be found in *The Second Isaiah: Introduction, Translation and Commentary to Chapters XL-LV*, which is being published by the Clarendon Press almost simultaneously with this second edition of the smaller work.

Some notes in the larger Commentary will appear to contradict those in the present work, which is reprinted exactly as it was published twelve years ago. But since it would never do to publish two books at the same time and on the same subject, and have the one contradicting the other, I have written a short Appendix embodying my more recent conclusions.

The reader may find some of the notes in the Appendix more difficult to understand than those in the original 'Torch'. This is partly because I have had to make them as brief as I can, and partly because they are based on points of Hebrew grammar which the novice may at times find difficult to follow. But since this book is (I know) used by university students who are learning Hebrew, I have been obliged to give reasons for opinions which may sometimes appear novel.

The notes in the Appendix should be read *together with*, not *instead of*, those in the original text, and the student is advised, before he begins to read, to make some sort of mark in the margins of the main work; otherwise he may overlook what is contained in the Appendix.

C. R. N.

Bangor
July, 1964

BIBLIOGRAPHY

BENTZEN, AAGE: *Jesaja fortolket*, Bind II, Copenhagen, 1948.

CHEYNE, T. K.: *The Prophecies of Isaiah*, vol. II, London, 1881, 5th ed., 1889.

DELITZSCH, F.: *Biblical Commentary on the Prophecies of Isaiah*, English Translation of 4th ed. by J. S. Banks and James Kennedy, Edinburgh, 1890.

DUHM, B.: *Das Buch Jesaia übersetzt und erklärt*, Göttingen, 1st ed., 1892, 4th ed., 1922.

FISCHER, J.: *Das Buch Isaias übersetzt und erklärt, II. Teil: Kapitel 40-66*, Bonn, 1939. (Catholic.)

KISSANE, E. J.: *The Book of Isaiah; Translated from a Critically Revised Hebrew Text with Commentary*, vol. II, Dublin, 1943. (Catholic.)

LEVY, R.: *Deutero-Isaiah: A Commentary*, Oxford, 1925. (Jewish.)

MUILENBERG, J.: 'The Book of Isaiah' (chapters 40-55), in *The Interpreter's Bible*, vol. V, New York and London, 1956, pp. 381-651.

NORTH, C. R.: *The Suffering Servant in Deutero-Isaiah*, 2nd ed., Oxford, 1956.

'The Interpretation of Deutero-Isaiah', in *Interpretationes ad Vetus Testamentum pertinentes* (Mowinckel Festschrift), Oslo, 1955, pp. 133-45. (Critique of Torrey and Simon.)

PEAKE, A. S.: *The Servant of Yahweh and other Lectures*, Manchester, 1931.

VAN DER PLOEG, J. S.: *Les Chants du Serviteur de Jahvé dans la seconde partie du livre d'Isaïe*, Paris, 1936. (Catholic.)

ROBINSON, H. W.: 'The Cross of the Servant', in *The Cross in the Old Testament*, London, 1955.

ROWLEY, H. H.: *The Servant of the Lord and Other Essays on the Old Testament*, London, 1952.

SIMON, U. E.: *A Theology of Salvation: A Commentary on Isaiah 40-55*, London, 1953.

SKINNER, J.: *The Book of the Prophet Isaiah Chapters XL-LXVI*, Cambridge, 1898, revised ed., 1917.

SMITH, G. A.: *The Book of Isaiah*, vol. II, London, 1890, 2nd ed., 1927.

SMITH, SIDNEY: *Isaiah Chapters XL-LV: Literary Criticism and History* (Schweich Lectures, 1940), London, 1944.

TORREY, C. C.: *The Second Isaiah: A New Interpretation*, Edinburgh, 1928.

VOLZ, P.: *Jesaja II übersetzt und erklärt*, Leipzig, 1932.

WADE, G. W.: *The Book of the Prophet Isaiah with Introduction and Notes*, Westminster Commentaries, London, 1911.

WARDLE, W. L.: 'Isaiah XL-LXVI', in *A Commentary on the Bible*, edited A. S. Peake, London and Edinburgh, 1924.

WHITEHOUSE, O. C.: *Isaiah XL-LXVI*, Century Bible, not dated.

ZIMMERLI, W. AND JEREMIAS, J.: *The Servant of God*, Eng. trans., London, 1957.

(For a full Bibliography see the author's *The Suffering Servant in Deutero-Isaiah*.)

INTRODUCTION

The middle section of the book of the Prophet Isaiah (chh. 40-55) is generally known as ' The Second Isaiah ' or, alternatively, ' Deutero-Isaiah '. This name for it dates only from the last quarter of the eighteenth century, when doubts began to be expressed whether the second half of Isaiah (chh. 40-66) was written by the prophet of that name. It had always been assumed that the book was a unity and that everything in it was the work of Isaiah of Jerusalem, whose ministry extended over the second half of the eighth century B.C. (roughly 750-700). That chh. 40-66 obviously refer to events two centuries later than Isaiah's own time occasioned no difficulty, since it was taken for granted that the prophets could, and did, predict events which were not to happen until long after they themselves were dead.

The belief in the unity of the book of Isaiah was current in N.T. times (see Matt. 3.3; Acts 8.30ff., where passages from ' Second Isaiah ' are quoted as from ' Isaiah '). It can even be traced back to the second century B.C. In the apocryphal book of Ecclesiasticus (written about 180 B.C.) there is a passage (Ecclus. 48.23f.) which reads, ' In his (Isaiah's) days the sun went backward; and he added life to the king. He saw by an excellent spirit what should come to pass at the last; and he comforted them that mourned in Zion. He shewed the things that should be to the end of time, and hidden things or ever they came.' This is clear evidence that the story of Hezekiah's sickness (Isa. 38), and what we now call Second Isaiah (cf. 40.1; 61.3), were already written on the same roll as Isa. 1-35. In other words, by about 200 B.C., at the latest, the book of Isaiah existed in the form in which we now have it. (It may be remarked that in the recently discovered Dead Sea Scrolls the whole of Isaiah is written on one manuscript. The date of the scrolls is not yet determined, but many believe they are pre-Christian.)

THE HISTORICAL BACKGROUND

In Isaiah's time the world-empire was Assyria, and the prophet pictured Assyria as a rod with which Yahweh would chastise his own people (10.5-15). In 612 Nineveh, the capital of Assyria, fell before an attack of Medes and Babylonians. In 605 the Egyptian Pharaoh, Necho II, was heavily defeated at Carchemish on the upper Euphrates, by the Babylonian Nebuchadrezzar, and the greater part of what had been the Assyrian Empire came under the control of a revived Babylonian (sometimes called the neo-Babylonian, sometimes the Chaldean) Empire, which lasted until 538. In 586 B.C. Jerusalem fell to the Babylonians; the Temple was destroyed and a large number of the inhabitants of Judah were deported to Babylon. Some years before 550 a new conqueror, a Persian named Cyrus, appeared in the east. After a series of spectacular victories, first over the Medes, then over Croesus of Lydia (547) and finally over the Babylonians, Cyrus entered Babylon in 538, and gave permission to the various peoples who had been deported there to return to their own countries.

It is agreed on all hands that the historical background of Isa. 40-55 is the career of Cyrus and the downfall of the Babylonian Empire. Cyrus is twice named in the prophecy (44.28; 45.1) and in other passages he is clearly referred to (41.2,25; 45.13; 46.11; 48.14f.). The Jews are in exile (42.22ff.; 48.20) in the land of the Chaldeans (47.5f.). Jerusalem and the cities of Judah are in ruins but are going to be rebuilt (44.26; 45.13; 52.2,9); likewise the Temple (44.28). Babylon, the proud mistress of kingdoms, is to be conquered (43.14; 46.1f.; 47) and the Jews are to return to their homeland (40.9ff.; 51.3). Even, therefore, if the chapters were written by Isaiah in the eighth century, it is against this sixth-century background that they must be interpreted.

DATE AND AUTHORSHIP

Were the chapters written by Isaiah, or by a prophet who lived in the sixth century, in the midst of the stirring events he describes? There is no need to deny that God could, if he would, predict events in detail two centuries in advance. The question is, does he do that? To ask that question is not to say that the prophets never predicted. They did. They were in the habit of predicting, and the statement that 'the prophets were not foretellers, but forthtellers' has been much overdone. But the predictions of a prophet were always fairly closely related to the circumstances of his own time, and it is difficult to see the relevance for Isaiah's time of *detailed* descriptions of happenings two centuries later. Prophets did, indeed, sometimes predict things which were not to happen for centuries, and which, for that matter, have not been fulfilled even yet (e.g. Isa. 2.4; 11.9), but when they did it was in general or 'mythological' (see below, p. 25ff.) terms. 'Second Isaiah' is still prediction, even if it is not by Isaiah of Jerusalem. But what it predicts is the rapidly approaching overthrow of Babylon and the release of the Jews from captivity. The exile, on the other hand, is not predicted, but presupposed, and the oppressor is not Assyria, as it was in Isaiah's time, but Babylon.

If anyone prefers to believe that Isaiah 40-55 was written by Isaiah of Jerusalem, he is perfectly free to do so, provided that be interprets it against its sixth-century background. In some ways it makes little difference. But there is one passage in the prophecy which seems definitely to rule out the possibility that it dates from the eighth century. It is 48.6f.: 'I have shewed thee new things from this time, even hidden things, which thou hast not known. They are created now, and not from of old; and before this day thou heardest them not; lest thou shouldest say, Behold, I knew them' (RV). If the 'new things' relate to the time of Cyrus, the words 'from this time', 'now', 'this day', can hardly relate to the time of Isaiah, for so the 'new things' would have been known for nearly two hundred

years, and it is definitely stated that 'before this day thou
heardest them not'. Nor may we appeal to Isaiah's words in
8.16, 'seal the law among my disciples'; that refers, not, as
in Dan. 12.4; Rev. 22.10 to a sealed *book*, but to oral 'teaching' (so RV marg.) which the prophet committed to his disciples and which would, therefore, be open to the members of
their circle.

There are other indications besides the historical background
which point to a later date than the eighth century. A
prominent element in the Prophet's teaching is his 'appeal to
prophecy' as it is often called (41.21-29; 43.9; 44.7f.). Yahweh,
he says, has in former times predicted things which have come
to pass; the heathen gods have nothing to set against this power
of his. Prophecy in Israel, it is true, goes back to the eleventh
century B.C., but prophecy of the kind that DI has in mind
dates, broadly, from the century of Isaiah, and the appeal to
it suggests a comparatively late date, when predictive prophecy
of world-wide import had an established reputation. Again,
the eighth-century Isaiah had denounced idols, called them
elilim, 'worthless nonentities' (2.8,18,20). The Second Isaiah
ridicules them (40.19f.; 41.6f.; 44.9-20). He pictures Yahweh
challenging them to meet him in the open forum of discussion
41.21-24). Let them do anything, either good or bad; let them
at least show some signs of animation and life! They are nothing at all! There is only one God, and he is Yahweh (45.5f.
and frequently). Monotheism is implicit in the teaching of the
eighth-century Isaiah; here it is explicit and absolute. Accordingly, in Isa. 40-55 there is more emphasis upon the creative
power of Yahweh (40.12-26) than there is in the earlier
chapters of the book. In a word, the theology of DI is more
developed than that of 'Proto'-Isaiah.

The language of Isa. 40-55, too, has features which make it
difficult to believe that it is Isaiah's, though this is an argument
difficult to appraise unless one reads Hebrew. But something
of it can be detected even in translation. Proto-Isaiah is
scintillating, brilliant, even torrential (see especially ch. 2).
Second Isaiah is sustained, rhetorical, magnificent, but it has

less impetuosity. Characteristic of it is the way in which, whenever Yahweh is named, the description of him is filled out with participial and other predicative phrases, as in 41.14; 43.14; 48.17—'Yahweh, thy redeemer, the Holy One of Israel'. (Similar examples, with variations of phrase, are 43.3; 44.6; 45.11; 54.5; 55.5—the attentive reader will discover others.) This 'hymnic' style, as it may be called, is comparatively rare in pre-exile poetry.

All things considered, then, it seems safe to conclude that Isa. 40-55 is the work of a prophet who lived in Babylonia during the middle years of the sixth century. In the closing verses of the prophecy (55.12f.) the release from Babylon appears still to lie in the future, so that it is probable that his work was finished before the return from exile. The beginning of his ministry almost certainly dates from a time after Cyrus set out on his career of conquest. The earliest of his oracles which can be fairly definitely dated is 41.1-5, and it fits in well with the early victories of Cyrus, up to the fall of Sardis, the capital of Lydia, and in the autumn of 547 B.C. Nothing is known of the person and fortunes of the prophet. He remains 'the great unknown'. Another designation of him, besides the Second or Deutero-Isaiah, is the 'Babylonian' Isaiah.

DEUTERO- AND TRITO-ISAIAH

Until 1892, when a German scholar named Duhm wrote a brilliant commentary on Isaiah, the name Deutero-Isaiah was given to the whole of the second part of the book (chh. 40-66). Although there are great similarities between 40-55 and 56-66, certain differences had long been noticed. The most obvious of them is that in some passages in 56-66 the Temple appears to be standing (56.5ff.; 60.7,13), though the walls of Jerusalem are not yet rebuilt (60.10). This suggests a date between the rebuilding of the Temple (516 B.C.) and the coming of Nehemiah to Jerusalem in 444. If we suppose that DI wrote the whole of

40-66, he must have returned to Palestine and exercised a long ministry there. Duhm proposed that 56-66 was the work of disciples of DI—this would explain the similarities of the two sections—and he gave it the name 'Trito-Isaiah'. It is only right to say that a few scholars still believe in the unity of 40-66. Some of those who distinguish between Deutero- and Trito-Isaiah think that the latter was one individual, but the more general opinion is that in Trito-Isaiah we have the work of a 'school' of 'disciples' of DI. Trito-Isaiah certainly gives the impression of being less of a unity than does DI. There is little in 40-55 which cannot with some confidence be assigned to the one author.

DEUTERO-ISAIAH AND PROTO-ISAIAH

How did it come about that DI was bound up with the work of Isaiah of Jerusalem? The most casual reader can hardly fail to note the similarities between Deutero- and Trito-Isaiah. There are also similarities, though they are less on the surface, between Deutero-and Proto-Isaiah. The most obvious is the epithet 'the Holy One of Israel' (1.4 + 11 times in Proto-, 41.14 + 10 times in Deutero-, and twice [60.9,14] in Trito-) and all that it implies for the 'Isaianic' conception of God. The expression is rare outside the book of Isaiah and Isaiah was the first to use it.

The forms in which the prophetical books have come down to us suggest strongly that they are not the literary creations of the men whose names they bear. Even Jewish tradition had it that 'Isaiah' was compiled by 'the men of Hezekiah'. This may not be an altogether accurate tradition, but it does point to a dim recollection on the part of the rabbis that a good deal of 'committee' work went to the editing of the prophetical books. Present-day critical opinion is that the words of the prophets were at first preserved, either orally or in writing or both, in the circles of their disciples. We read (8.16) of Isaiah committing his teaching to his disciples. There are good reasons for supposing that the circles of disciples of a master-prophet could continue for generations, during which time materials more or less in the style of the master would become attached to the original deposit of his teaching and be current under his name. Thus, there are passages in Proto-Isaiah which have a distinctly Deutero-Isaianic ring: examples are 13f., a taunt-song on the fall of Babylon, not unlike 47; and 35, which is so like DI that some scholars have supposed that it actually comes from him. These associations of disciples of a master-prophet kept alive faith and hope, and sometimes —in the case of the Isaiah-circle, nearly two centuries later— a 'revival' would break out within the circle. Thus a Deutero-Isaiah, moved by the world-shaking events of his time, would raise anew the torch which had first been kindled by Isaiah, and the torch would continue to burn even during the rather dreary days—as they turned out to be—of the first return from exile. What goes under the name of Isaiah is the fruit of three centuries of faith and witness, inaugurated by Isaiah in the eighth century, and renewed by an unnamed sixth-century prophet who had all the originality and sublimity of the founder of the circle. We should like to have known his name, but his own name meant nothing to him compared with the declaration of the word which God gave him to utter.

It should perhaps be added that 39.5-8 is often regarded as a formal link between 1-39 and 40-66, and those who plead for the Isaianic authorship of the whole book say that 40-66 is a perfectly natural amplification of what Isaiah said to Hezekiah. This argument might have more cogency were it not that 36-39 are, with some modifications, the same as II Kings 18.13-20.19. It looks as if the original 'book' of Isaiah ended, like Jeremiah (cf. Jer. 52 with II Kings 24.18-25.30) with an excerpt from II Kings. Ch. 39 was not, therefore, written purposely as a preparation for 40-66.

THE FORM OF THE PROPHECY

It is usual to divide the prophecy into two more or less equal halves, 40-48 and 49-55. Not that 49-55 is from a different author from 40-48, but the emphasis is upon a different set of thoughts. In 40-48 the emphasis is upon the advent of Cyrus. In 49-55 it is upon the restoration of Israel and the rehabilitation of Zion; no more do we hear of the unfolding of political and military events, of the argument from prophecy, of the career of Cyrus and the fall of Babylon. It has sometimes been thought that the Prophet composed 49-55 after the return to Palestine. But since the return is still depicted as future (51.14; 52.11f.; 55.12f.), it seems better to conclude that the whole is earlier than the return, though 49-55 may have been composed later than 40-48.

With the possible exception of one or two passages, the whole of the prophecy is in poetry. There is no rhyme in Hebrew poetry—only occasional assonance—nor does the line contain a fixed number of syllables, though it does, as a rule, contain a definite number of stresses or accented syllables. The most characteristic feature of Hebrew poetry is what is known as 'parallelism', which is easily recognizable in translation. To take an example at random:

> Seék ye the LÓRD while he may be found,
> Cáll ye upon him while he is néar:
> Let the wícked forsáke his wáy,
> And the unrighteous mán his thoúghts:
> And let him retúrn unto the LÓRD, and he will
>   have mércy upon him;
> And to our Gód, for he will abúndantly párdon.
>
> (55.6f.)

(The stresses in the Hebrew are indicated by acute accents.) In this passage lines 2, 4, and 6, repeat in different words the thoughts of lines 1, 3, and 5. The prevailing rhythm is roughly anapaestic.

Unlike most prophecies (e.g. Proto-Isaiah and Jeremiah), DI contains no biographical or autobiographical materials. It consists entirely of prophetic utterances. In these the Prophet is represented as speaking on behalf of God, as the very mouthpiece of God, and the personal pronoun 'I' almost invariably stands for God, not for the Prophet himself. In pre-exilic prophecy the single prophetic utterance or 'oracle' was usually quite short, of an average length of five or six verses. Whether that holds good also for DI, which has more of the character of written prophecy, is still a matter for discussion, though the majority opinion is that the prophecy contains some fifty separate units. These separate units have no necessary or logical connexion with one another, but—again according to the general opinion—have been brought together on two main principles of association. The first principle is that of similarity of subject-matter: e.g. passages relating to Cyrus are all found in chh. 40-48 and a certain rough chronological order is discernible throughout the prophecy. The second principle is a kind of 'domino' or 'catchword' principle: e.g. oracles beginning with 'Hearken unto me' (51.1,4,7) or 'Awake, awake' (51.9,17; 52.1) are grouped more or less together. Some scholars dissent from the 'small units' theory, and hold instead that the prophecy was constructed according to a definite literary pattern and that the number of separate 'units' or (better) 'complexes', may be fewer than ten. It has even been suggested in recent years that the prophecy was framed after the pattern of a liturgy, though this is not intended to mean that it was written to be used as a liturgy. Whether that is so it is difficult to say with any confidence, since we know little of the forms of ancient Hebrew liturgies, at least of any length. All that can be said is that DI bears more of the marks of a single editorial mind than any other prophetical writing, except perhaps Malachi.

In the English RV the prophecy is divided into fifty-four paragraphs, but it must not be supposed that these paragraphs agree with the 'some fifty' units into which the majority of scholars to-day would divide the book. For example, 52.13-

53.12 is almost unanimously regarded as one unit, but it is divided into five paragraphs in the RV. No two scholars agree on the exact divisions, or even on the number of the units. In this commentary the unit of exposition will be the paragraph, and the divisions into paragraphs will be those which appeal most to the judgment of the writer. They are not intended to be authoritative or final, and the reader is free to make his own divisions if he chooses.

THE FULFILMENT OF THE PROPHECY

(Before studying this section of the Introduction, the reader is recommended to read through the prophecy at one sitting, so as to obtain a bird's-eye view of its contents.)

The prophecy is predominantly ' eschatological ', i.e. it has to do with ' the last things '; not ' the last things ' as they are expounded in Christian theology, but as the Hebrew Prophet of the sixth century B.C. expected them to unfold. If we may use the N.T. phrase ' the kingdom of God '—though the Prophet does not use precisely that expression—what is described is the coming of the kingdom of God. That kingdom is to come soon, with the fall of Babylon and the return of the exiles to their homeland, and its coming is to be complete and final. Yahweh is to lead his people home, not by the caravan way which Abraham took when he travelled from Babylonia to Canaan *via* Harran and North Syria, but direct across the North Arabian desert. The exiles are to travel in comfort: their march is to be like the triumphal procession of a military conqueror, with the victorious Yahweh himself at their head. Valleys are to be exalted, mountains and hills levelled; rivers are to flow in the desert, and along their banks will be forest trees. It is to be a second and more wonderful Exodus, accompanied by a complete transformation of nature. The heathen are to see and acknowledge the glory of Yahweh, and Cyrus is to recognize that it is Yahweh who has given him his victories.

Are we to take all this literally? Did the Prophet himself intend it to be taken literally? It is not easy to say, but there are several considerations to be borne in mind. In the first place, what the Prophet uttered was not prose, but impassioned poetry. Even so, he certainly expected something very wonderful to happen, something which could only be expressed in poetry and for which prose was quite inadequate. Whether we take his words literally or not, then, is comparatively unimportant; clearly, he expected something supernatural to happen. In the next place, no one in ancient times—least of all a prophet—had any hesitation about believing that the supernatural could, and did, happen. The Hebrews did not make the sharp distinction between natural and supernatural that we do. They had not brought everything under the control of 'natural laws'. They accepted 'miracles' as a matter of course. Certainly, when God came, miracles would happen. Further, although there was a material element in the Prophet's expectations, it is not grossly material. We should remember, too, that in the sixth century B.C. there was no general belief in a future life for the individual; indeed, God's dealings were primarily with the nation Israel rather than with the individual Israelite. We may, therefore, ask how the favour of God could be manifested to the nation without some emphasis upon physical blessings. Even so, the physical blessings were not regarded as things to be enjoyed simply for their own sake; they were rather the evidences of the good pleasure of God.

It would seem, then, that the Prophet expected Yahweh to come in all the plenitude of his grace and power, and that his coming would be accompanied by a permanent physical and moral transformation of the world. Even if we take the poetic language as figurative, and translate it into prose, it still remains that the Prophet believed that the world was standing upon the threshold of a decisive manifestation of God in history. What became of these high expectations? It must be admitted that they were very imperfectly realized. Babylon fell, and Cyrus gave permission to the Jews, amongst other peoples, to return to their homes. As his decree is reported in the O.T. (II Chron.

36.23; Ezra 1.2ff.) it reads as if he acknowledged Yahweh as the only God and giver of victory to him. But since there is extant an actual inscription of Cyrus in which he attributes his victories to the favour of the Babylonian god Marduk, it would seem that the Bible version of his decree has been coloured by the patriotic monotheism of the Jews, perhaps even by the terms of DI's expectations of him. Certainly he did not become in any sense a convert to the Jewish faith, nor was there any widespread conversion of the Gentiles.

There is no reason to doubt that some Jews did avail themselves of the permission of Cyrus to return to Palestine in or shortly after 538. Their leader was one Sheshbazzar (Ezra 1.8), about whom nothing further is known. They were probably a small company. Ezra 2 speaks of 42,360 'which came with Zerubbabel, Jeshua, Nehemiah' and others (v. 2, note the comma after Zerubbabel in RV, not colon as in AV). We know that Zerubbabel was in Jerusalem in 520 (cf. Hag. and Zech. 1-8); but since the list is duplicated in Neh. 7.6-73, and contains the names of Nehemiah, who returned in 444, and proselytes with Babylonian and Persian names (Mordecai and Bigvai), it would seem that it includes all those who returned during the century or more following 538. No serious attempt was made to rebuild the Temple until the prophets Haggai and Zechariah urged the people to it in 520. The rebuilding of the walls of Jerusalem had to wait until it was undertaken, against serious opposition, by Nehemiah. Trito-Isaiah and Malachi, which are best referred to the period between the dedication of the Temple (516) and the advent of Nehemiah, are clear evidence that the century following the first meagre 'return', was a time of disillusionment and hope deferred. The Jerusalem Jews were poor and dispirited; they had much ado to keep their faith alive amid the heathenism with which they were surrounded; and in order to preserve it at all they cast it into a mould of legalism which, on the whole, made them sour and uncharitable in their attitude to non-Jews.

Even, therefore, if we translate DI's physical imagery into spiritual terms, it is clear that his glowing expectations were only partially realized. Are we, then, to set him down as a deluded enthusiast, making 'a leap into the pure blue and away from facts'? It is no way to save his reputation as a prophet simply to say that his expectations would have been fulfilled if only his fellow-Jews had not been so inert and stupid. What was to be expected of the average Jewish exile, or, indeed, of average human nature in any age? During this century we ourselves have passed through two world wars, in each of which we buoyed ourselves up with the confidence that all would be well when the wars were over. It is not exactly that stupid people stand in the way of the realization of prophetic dreams. It is rather that our human times are in the hand of God. Life is as we have known it, and as the Jews knew it in the sixth and fifth centuries B.C. Even so, practical men of action like Nehemiah and Ezra seem much more realistic and sensible than exuberant prophets like DI. Is that all that is to be said about the matter? Or are we to say that DI's teaching about the nature of God is still magnificent and full of inspiration even though for the rest we write him down as an impracticable idealist? That will hardly do, since the Prophet based his descriptions of what God is *like* upon what he expected God to *do*. And if God did not do what the Prophet expected he would, have we any assurance that God is what the Prophet thought he was? We are face to face with a real, indeed a contemporary problem: millions of people to-day have a reverence for Christianity; they would like to believe it true, but with the best will in the world they cannot; the facts of life seem dead against it. Must we, then, 'debunk' DI?

Is it possible that the Prophet lived long enough to discover his own 'mistake', and that he did some 'debunking' of himself? There is reason to believe that his descriptions of the Suffering Servant (42.1-4; 49.1-6; 50.4-9; 52.13-53.12) are intended as in some sort a foil to Cyrus. Even so, we are left wondering why his earlier 'mistaken' enthusiasms are bound up not only with his own more 'mature' thought—if we like to call it so—but with the whole body of Scripture. What is

more—and here we begin to see some solution to our problem
—the N.T. Gospels take their cue, at their very beginnings,
from the beginning of the gospel of DI (Matt. 3.3; Mark 1.3;
Luke 3.4ff.; cf. Isa. 40.3), just as Handel's *Messiah* does. Quite
clearly, DI looked forward to something very wonderful. To
say that nothing of what he expected happened, would be an
exaggeration; still, the immediate sequel was disappointing.
Equally clearly, something very wonderful did happen when
Christ came, and that something was related, both by the
evangelists and by Jesus himself, to what DI had predicted.
In particular, Jesus said that Isa. 61.1-2, which is altogether
Deutero-Isaianic in tone, and which for him was as much
'Isaiah' as everything else in the book, was fulfilled in himself (Luke 4.16-21); he also read the passages about the Suffering Servant as referring to himself. Either, then, DI was an
impossible dreamer—a not very satisfying proposition—or
what he dreamed took shape in the life, death, and resurrection
of Jesus, as the N.T. says it did. On a short view, his prophecy
was largely unfulfilled; on the long view it was more than fulfilled, it was exceeded. His kingdom of God did come; it came
when Jesus came. That it came six centuries later, and not
within a decade, is little matter. The view of any great prophet
is 'foreshortened'. He sees, inevitably, and with almost blind-
ing intensity, the consummation as something near at hand.
What he sees is not a photographic description of the future,
but something which, in the sequel, exceeds in glory (cf. II Cor.
3.9) his necessarily imperfect vision.

THE INTERPRETATION OF THE
PROPHECY

From what has been said in the preceding section it would seem
that we are justified in giving a 'mythological' interpretation
to the prophecy, both to the Prophet's descriptions of the
approaching exodus from Babylon and to the sufferings of the
Servant. Indeed, a mythological interpretation is not only

justified; if there is anything more in the prophecy than pure vapourings, such an interpretation seems absolutely necessary. But first, it should be explained that a 'myth' is not just any fanciful or untrue story. Myths are related in all seriousness. They may relate to the past, or they may relate to the future. Let us take a myth relating to the past: it is clear that something is radically wrong with human nature. Human nature is sinful. How did it come to be sinful? Any answer to that question must take the form of a 'myth', since whatever it was that happened, happened before the age of recorded history. A myth may be told about something that happened before the dawn of recorded history, in order to explain a situation with which we are confronted and which must have come about somehow. Such a myth is the story of the Fall in Gen. 3. It is not history, but it is psychologically convincing; it still speaks to the conscience of men who are willing to be awakened from their moral slumbers, and it is unlikely that, in its own way, it will ever be improved upon.

A myth may also refer to the future. It is then a description of something which lies beyond the horizons of any future that we can envisage, or even of something actually existing but which we cannot see clearly from where we stand now. When we say of Christ in the Apostles' Creed that 'he sitteth at the right hand of God the Father Almighty; from whence he shall come to judge the quick and the dead', we are speaking the language of mythology. We know that Christ is not dead, but alive, and this is an attempt to describe what he is doing now and what he will do at the consummation of all things. Or when the seer in the N.T. Apocalypse wishes to describe the glories of heaven, he can only do it in mythological terms (Rev. 21f.).

The Second Isaiah lived at a crisis in the history of his people. Something was about to happen. He described in mythological language what he expected would happen. What he depicted was in more glowing terms than anything which happened in his own lifetime, but it was even transcended by what did happen six centuries later. To call the Prophet a doting enthusiast is to do him much less than justice. He, more than any other prophet, is the evangelist of the O.T., and the N.T. accords him that honour. We, too, can accord him no less. What Canon Alan Richardson has written ('The Gospel in the N.T.', in *The Enduring Gospel*, edited by R. Gregor Smith, 1950, pp. 36f.) is true: 'The N.T. writers do not think of themselves as replacing the O.T. but rather as re-interpreting it in the light of its true fulfilment. They did not even call it " the Old Testament ", because it was the only sacred Scripture that they knew. They were conscious rather that now for the first time it was possible to read and understand the Hebrew Scriptures aright. What had formerly been only a partially revealed mystery could now be correctly interpreted; the dark secrets of the Law, the Prophets and the Writings could now be brought into the light. That light had been shed by the appearing in the flesh of Jesus, the Messiah. The times of fulfilment had arrived, and what the Scriptures of the O.T. had themselves prophesied had now come to pass. . . . It was therefore now possible to understand the Scriptures in their true meaning, as the Jews of former days could never have understood them, because the interpreting Spirit revealed their secrets and made clear in all the Scriptures the things concerning Christ.'

As recently as a generation ago a commentator was considered to have done his duty if he explained exactly what a Scripture writer meant when he wrote what he did, that and nothing more. This was a necessary corrective to the centuries-old habit of interpreting allegorically, in what might be entire disregard of what was immediately in the mind of the original writer. True, we must still begin with what a writer meant in the historical situation in which he lived. But, particularly in the case of 'the evangelist of the O.T.', we are permitted, indeed we seem required, to interpret what he wrote in the context of Scripture as a whole, reading the promise in the light of its fulfilment. This was the method of the N.T. itself when interpreting the Old, and, with due discrimination, it ought to be ours. 'With due discrimination': two cautions may be entered, lest the reader should expect too much, and be disappointed at not finding more. (1) The prophecy of DI is more than usually pregnant with meaning and a full commentary on its original meaning could fill a substantial volume. Considerations of space make it impossible to do more than set up sign-posts to indicate the directions Christian exposition should take. (2) A commentary which sets out to be 'Christian' can easily become merely homiletical and it is no business of a commentator to preach sermons. The reader can do much to help himself if he follows up the marginal references and makes use of a good concordance. Exposition is largely concordance work. Finally, it may be remarked that great hymn-writers like Isaac Watts and Charles Wesley are, in their own way, incomparably the finest commentators. The reader should note correspondences between the language of Scripture and the hymns he sings. He will then discover how O.T. themes and language have been wrought into the texture of Christian devotion.

THE SUFFERING SERVANT

(The reading of this paragraph should be preceded by a study of the notes on 'The Servant Songs', 42.1-4; 49.1-6; 50.4-9; 52.13-53.12.)

The question of the identity of the Suffering Servant has received a bewildering variety of answers. The views put forward may be summarized as follows:

A. Jewish Interpretations. At the beginning of the Christian era there were some who identified the Servant with 'the righteous' or 'the wise' of their own community. This interpretation was based upon Dan. 12.3, where 'they that are wise' and are to 'turn many to righteousness' (Heb. lit. 'justify many') seems distinctly reminiscent of 52.13 and 53.11. Quite early in the Christian era there were Jews who identified the Servant with the Messiah, though this interpretation was never con-

sistently applied, since it was no part of Jewish expectation
that the Messiah son of David would suffer. Accordingly, and
largely as a reaction from the Christian claim that the Servant was Jesus, the view gradually prevailed that he was the
Jewish nation. This is the general Jewish view.

B. Christian Interpretations. From the very beginning Christians interpreted Isa. 53 as a prophecy of Christ. There is
abundant evidence for this in the N.T. (e.g. Acts 8.27-39; I Pet.
2.22-25), and there seems no doubt that Jesus read the passage
as pointing to himself (e.g. Mark 1.11 [see note on 42.1];
10.45 [see note on 53.12]). Until the end of the eighteenth
century there was scarcely any dissent from this view, the only
notable exception being the Dutch scholar, Grotius, who
said that 52.13-53.12 referred to Jeremiah, 'as a figure of
Christ'.

(i) COLLECTIVE INTERPRETATION. When, at the end of the
eighteenth century, Isa. 40-55 came to be detached from 1-39
and assigned to a prophet of the exile, it no longer seemed
compelling to regard the chapters as long-range prediction.
Accordingly, an increasing number of Christian scholars
adopted the Jewish view that the Servant was the nation
Israel. This seemed reasonable because in several passages
in DI Israel is actually called Yahweh's Servant (see notes on
42.1-4). The fact that the Servant does not, like Israel, suffer
for his own sins, but for the sins of others, and that his patience
under suffering is in marked contrast to the querulousness of
Israel in the main prophecy, was an obvious difficulty for the
'full collective theory'. This difficulty, it was thought, could
be obviated, or at any rate minimized, by identifying the Servant with a pious remnant of faithful Israelites, or with the
order of prophets. Another suggestion has been to equate him
with the 'ideal' as distinct from the 'real', i.e. historical Israel.
Neither of these expedients is altogether satisfactory. The
sufferings of the exile came upon all the exiles alike; it was not
that a minority suffered for the rest, while the rest escaped. As
for 'ideal' Israel, the O.T. knows little of any distinction

between 'ideal' and 'real', and it is difficult to see how an 'ideal' Israel could be said to suffer at all.

The most attractive form of the collective theory is that associated with the name of the late Principal H. Wheeler Robinson, who stressed the importance of 'corporate personality' for the understanding of the O.T. According to this, Hebrew thought could pass easily and naturally from the community to the individual and back again. The individual ancestor was the embodiment of the people descended from him, and Israel could be addressed as 'you' or 'thou', sometimes with abrupt transition from the plural to the singular and vice versa. Accordingly there was expansion and contraction, 'systole and diastole', in the Prophet's idea of the Servant; hence it was quite possible for 'Israel' to have a mission to 'Israel' (cf. 49.1-6), very much as faithful Christians can have a mission to the Church. While, therefore, the Prophet always thought of the Servant as Israel, the effective Servant could be contracted to one individual, the Prophet himself.

(ii) HISTORICAL INDIVIDUAL THEORIES. There are many such theories and they may be divided into three groups.

(a) *Theories which identify the Servant with an individual who had lived in the near or distant past*. Among the individuals for whom claims have been made are Hezekiah, Uzziah, Isaiah, Jeremiah, Zerubbabel, Meshullam the son of Zerubbabel (see note on 42.19 and cf. I Chron. 3.19), Jehoiachin, Moses, and even Cyrus. Identifications with Hezekiah, Uzziah and Isaiah presuppose that the passages are from Proto-Isaiah. Those with Hezekiah, Uzziah, Zerubbabel, Jehoiachin, Meshullam, and even Moses, are semi-Messianic, since all were kings (actual or prospective) or rulers. The theory that the Servant was Moses was based upon a speculation that Moses had been murdered by his own countrymen, a speculation which necessitated drastic conjectural emendation of passages in the book of Hosea, of all places! Of all these named-individual theories, that which would see in Jeremiah the model for the Servant is the most attractive. There are undoubtedly features of Jeremiah in the portrait (see on 49.1:

53.7), but that he *was* the Servant intended by the Prophet is impossible to maintain, if only because, although he suffered, he did not suffer patiently. Moreover, the Servant not only suffered *as a consequence of* his mission; suffering was *the means* whereby he was to bring his mission to a successful issue. It is sufficient to say that these theories, fixing as they do upon individuals so diverse in character and calling, cancel one another out, and that none of them has any serious backing to-day.

(*b*) *Historico-Messianic Theory.* One or two scholars have suggested that the Servant was an anonymous contemporary of the Prophet, a seer who, the Prophet believed, was destined to be the Messiah. The Prophet ' discovered ' him, so to speak, and encouraged him to undertake the political restoration of Israel, a course which brought him into conflict with the Babylonian authorities and resulted in his violent death. It is a fatal objection to this theory that the Prophet, of all men, deflected the Servant from a spiritual to a political vocation, and so, in effect, became his evil genius.

(*c*) *Autobiographical Theory.* Rather more than thirty years ago the suggestion was put forward in all seriousness that the Servant was none other than the Prophet, DI himself (cf. Acts 8.34). The objection to this theory is that it would require us to suppose that the Prophet-Servant composed his own obituary. A modification of the theory is that the last Song was composed by a disciple of the Prophet (Trito-Isaiah) as a threnody on his martyred master. This is highly conjectural and speculative. It is one thing to say that the portrait of the Servant contains features of the Prophet, as it undoubtedly does; it is quite another to say that the Prophet intended the Songs as a self-portrait.

(iii) MYTHOLOGICAL INTERPRETATION. The suggestion has been widely made in recent years that the figure of the Servant is related to the myth of the dying and rising god (Tammuz). The obvious objection to this is that Tammuz was a nature god pure and simple, and that his death had no atoning significance. That there are occasional features of Tammuz in the portrait of the Servant (notably in 53.2,10ff.) is not improbable. This may be conceded even by those who hold to the traditional Messianic interpretation. To say that the Servant *is* Tammuz or any other cultic mythological figure is quite another matter, and no one has the hardihood to maintain it.

(iv) MESSIANIC INTERPRETATION. This may take a number of forms. Even since the end of the eighteenth century there have always been scholars who have maintained the traditional Messianic interpretation. More often than not they have been 'fundamentalists' who have insisted upon the unity of the book of Isaiah. Since the end of the nineteenth century, however, there have been those who have admitted the sixth-century date of Isa. 40-55, but have nevertheless seen in the Servant an individual figure whom the Prophet expected still to come. Some of them have identified him with the Messianic king of the line of David; others have regarded him as a soteriological rather than a royal figure, a 'Messiah of the exile' rather than a political Messiah. The latest form of Messianic interpretation is one which would relate the sufferings of the Servant to certain ritual 'sufferings' or penances which, there is some reason to believe, the Davidic king had to undergo annually at the New Year festival. (For further particulars see the writer's article 'The Suffering Servant: Recent Scandinavian Discussions', in *The Scottish Journal of Theology*, iii, 1950, pp. 363-79.)

An examination of the language of the Songs leaves little doubt that DI was their author. This is not quite so obvious for the last Song as it is for the other three; nevertheless, the Song is more like the work of DI than that of any other O.T. writer.

The picture of the Servant in the Songs is not entirely consistent. The conclusion of the first Song (42.4) seems definitely to exclude any prospect of an ignominious death, and even in the third (50.7-9), near as its situation obviously is to the final tragedy, the Servant is confident. True, in the sequel his confidence has been justified, but not in the simple way he had expected, by divine intervention. These differences may be due to the dramatic skill of the writer, who presented four scenes, each a sequel to the preceding, but with a time-interval. In other words, the Prophet knew the end from the beginning, but presented his scenes in such a way that each would introduce an element of surprise, not unmixed with perplexity, to his readers. Another and more likely explanation of the inconsistencies is that the Prophet himself only gradually entered into 'the burthen of the mystery', that his vision became clearer with each successive revelation to him. This would explain why the pieces are distributed at intervals in the prophecy. That they were composed after, rather than before, the main prophecy is practically certain. Had they been composed earlier, the leading thought in them, that of vicarious suffering, must surely have shown itself also in the main prophecy. It is likely that the new revelation which was vouchsafed to the Prophet came to him after the disappointment he must have experienced in Cyrus. He, too, learned obedience by the things which he suffered (Heb. 5.8). This would explain why the first Song is placed, by way of contrast, in a Cyrus context, while the others are in the second half of the prophecy, after Cyrus has made his exit.

Who, then, was the Servant? We must obviously begin where the Prophet himself began, with the equation the Servant = Israel (41.8, etc.). But to accept the collective interpretation as the final word, even in its attractive corporate personality form, is open to serious difficulties. Why should the Servant outside the Songs always be called Jacob-Israel, while in the Songs (except in 49.3, on which see note) he is anonymous? Moreover, the anonymity of the Servant in the Songs is accompanied by increasingly heightened individualization in the portrait of him, until it is difficult not to think that in the last Song the Prophet had in mind an individual. The character of the Servant, too, is different in the Songs from that of Israel in the main prophecy. Even if the Prophet was himself unconscious of these differences, they must have some significance. A further very obstinate difficulty is that on the collective theory all the hindrances and disappointments of the Servant in the earlier Songs, and his manifold sufferings and death in the last, are so many allegorical representations of the exile. There is no movement from the situations in the earlier Songs to the final climax in the last. Instead of a real drama we have a series of tableaux depicting the same situation.

Quite apart from the concept of corporate personality, the fact that so many and so diverse solutions of the problem have been attempted, suggests that the picture is a composite one. Many prophets and kings have contributed to it. This is the element of truth in the historical-individual theories. Yet when we have gathered them all together, we are left with a *plus* unaccounted for. Further, to say that the picture is composite means that the Servant is an ideal rather than an actual figure, that for DI he existed so far in imagination rather than in actual fact. This is borne out by the last Song, in which the Servant is visited by almost every imaginable indignity and suffering (see the notes on the passage). Also, there are hints that his sufferings, although represented as past, actually lie in the future (see note on 53.11).

According to the corporate personality theory the individual to whom the Servant contracts is the undifferentiated Prophet himself. It is much more probable that the Prophet thought of an individual still to come, one who would, in his own person, fully actualize the Servant ideal. The Songs are provisional or anticipated history, mythological in the sense of the word described above (p. 27). They are not photographic descriptions of the Christ who came six centuries later, but their general similarity, even to many details, is astonishing. Jesus recognized them as pointing to himself and they served to guide them in his predestined way (cf. Mark 14.21).

Christian interpreters, including those who accept the corporate personality solution, are unanimous that whoever the Servant was as the Prophet intended to portray him, Jesus crucified and risen alone responds adequately to the picture of his person and work. One of the most famous symbols suggested in the long debate on the problem is that of Franz

Delitzsch, who likened the Servant conception to a pyramid with Israel as its base and Christ as its apex. Any horizontal line drawn through the pyramid would represent a pious nucleus, larger or smaller, of Israelites. An extension of the figure would give a graph somewhat like this:

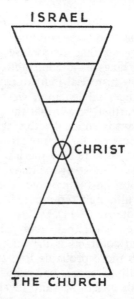

ISRAEL

CHRIST

THE CHURCH

The Christian Church is the heir to the Servant vocation of Israel in the O.T. The intermediate horizontal lines represent faithful nuclei, of Jews under the Old, of Christians under the New Covenant.

I

ISAIAH 40

COMFORT MY PEOPLE
40.1-2

These verses of comfort are the keynote of the prophecy. An earlier prophet of judgement had given to one of his children the name Lo-ammi ('not my people', Hos. 1.9), in token that Yahweh had rejected his people, though he had prophesied that Yahweh would one day return to them in mercy and once more call them 'my people' (Hos. 2.23). That time had now come. *MY* PEOPLE, *YOUR* GOD: the words are at once a fulfilment of earlier prophecy, an assurance for the present, and a promise for the future. The repeated COMFORT YE, COMFORT YE is characteristic of the style of DI (cf. 'Awake, awake', 51.9,17; 52.1). It makes assurance doubly sure. The words are spoken by the Prophet, at Yahweh's bidding (SAITH YOUR GOD), to others who are to repeat the proclamation in chorus. Who these others are is not said and it is perhaps vain to inquire. It may be that the Prophet is thinking not so much of different voices in unison but of the cumulative immensity of the comfort (CRY UNTO HER). Jerusalem was hundreds of miles away, but the message of comfort was as much for the exiles in Babylon as it was for the mother-city in the homeland. JERUSALEM, personified as a woman, is almost parallel with MY PEOPLE. It stands, in DI, not only for a geographical location, but for an idea, the community of God's people, the kingdom of God. In the language of Christian devotion it has become almost synonymous with the Church, as in James Montgomery's hymn:

> *Pray for Jerusalem,*
> *The city of our God;*
> *The Lord from heaven be kind to them*
> *That love the dear abode!*

2. Speak ye comfortably to

Lit. 'speak to the heart of'. The expression is found eight
times in the O.T. (Gen. 34.3; 50.21; Judg. 19.3; Ruth 2.13;
II Sam. 19.7; II Chron. 30.22; Hos. 2.14, and here), in five of
them of the wooing of a lover. The Hosea passage is again
significant: Hosea (Hos. 2.15-20) and Jeremiah (Jer. 2.2) had
pictured Israel as the bride of Yahweh. This figure is taken
up in DI (54.1-8) and is continued even into the N.T. in the
conception of the Church as the bride of Christ (Rev. 19.7;
21.2,9).

her warfare is accomplished

Better 'her bondservice is ended'; cf. Job 7.1, where 'warfare'
(RV, marg. 'time of service') is parallel with 'the days of an
hireling'.

her iniquity is pardoned

Better 'her punishment is accepted' (RV marg.) or 'her
penalty is discharged'. The Hebrew word for 'iniquity' serves
also, by metonymy, for the guilt that attaches to iniquity and to
the punishment that follows it.

double for all her sins

The prophets never thought of the exile as due to political
misfortune, the fate of a small nation doomed to extinction
at the hands of a powerful aggressor, but as a penalty for
sin, RECEIVED OF YAHWEH'S HAND. The DOUBLE is not something that Jerusalem is to receive as compensation for her
sufferings; it is something she has already suffered. We must
not read into it that Yahweh has inflicted punishment twice
as heavy as was deserved. The prophet of comfort is speaking

to the children of those whom his predecessors had denounced
so severely. *They* have suffered ' enough '.

PREPARE THE WAY OF THE LORD
40.3-5

The Prophet hears a celestial voice summoning angelic
ministers to prepare a processional highway for the return to
Jerusalem. Ezekiel had described Yahweh's departure, alone,
from the doomed city (Ezek. 11.22-25). Now he is to return
in public triumph, bringing the exiles with him. The description is intended literally, of physical, not moral hindrances.
The route is to lie straight across the desert between Babylon
and Palestine. Valleys are to be raised, mountains levelled,
and every hindrance put out of the way. THE GLORY OF
YAHWEH, of which Ezekiel had been the sole witness when
it departed from the city, is to be revealed for all mankind
(ALL FLESH) to see. Any lingering doubts that may have
remained after the first words of comfort are dispelled by the
assurance, FOR THE MOUTH OF YAHWEH HATH SPOKEN IT.
Notice how the verses rise to a crescendo. This is to be dis-
cerned, not only in the emotional content of the lines but even
in their length, and something of it is preserved even in
translation, literally:

> *Hark! One is crying,*
> *In the wilderness prepare the way of Yahweh,*
> *Make level in the desert a highway for our God.*

The parallelism is perfect: the comma should stand after
CRIETH (as in RV), not after WILDERNESS. The punctuation
in the Gospels (Mark 1.3) follows that of the LXX, which
seemed to point to John the Baptist, who appeared in the
wilderness as the herald of Jesus.

GOD'S PROMISE STANDS FOR EVER SURE
40.6-8

אמר ז
LXX

The Prophet hears another celestial voice bidding him
CRY! He asks WHAT SHALL I CRY? He is answered that man
is but grass (cf. Ps. 90.5f.; 103.15f.). His GOODLINESS (? 'devotion', perhaps 'charm' or 'beauty'—there is some uncertainty
about the precise meaning of the word here) is as evanescent as
the flower which fades. By contrast, the word of God shall
stand for ever.

6. The voice said, Cry
Again, 'Hark! One saying, Cry.'

And he said
Read 'And I said', with LXX and DSI. It is the only passage in which the Prophet speaks explicitly of himself, though
the paragraphs beginning with vv. 1 and 3 contain words which
he, so to say, overheard in the celestial council, as Isaiah
heard voices in his temple vision (Isa. 6).

7. the spirit of the LORD
Better 'breath' (RV) or 'wind'. The Hebrew word *ruach* can
mean either 'wind' or 'spirit'. The whole verse is omitted
in LXX and Vulgate, and in DSI has been entered between
the lines and in the margin by another copyist. It may be a
later insertion. The rather prosy SURELY THE PEOPLE IS GRASS
is almost certainly not original.

THE GOOD SHEPHERD
40.9-11

The procession now reaches the environs of Jerusalem. The
inhabitants of the city are to make their way up to a high
mountain, probably the Mount of Olives (cf. 22.1f. which

speaks of the city as 'wholly gone up to the housetops'). There they are to lift up their voice WITH STRENGTH, undeterred by any fear of Babylonian espionage or by any lingering want of faith. Voices in hilly country travel far (cf. Judg. 9.7; I Sam. 26.13f.), and orientals can make their voices very penetrating. The cry is to go out to the 'daughter' cities of Jerusalem, BEHOLD YOUR GOD! The gaze of the beholders will be fixed, not upon the returning exiles, but upon *God* (an amazing anthropomorphism!). *He* is the centre of the picture. Two qualities he displays, strength and gentleness. Both are combined in the figure of the shepherd. The Israelite king was the shepherd of his people, and wherever in the O.T. the word 'shepherd' is used figuratively, it is always of a ruler (cf. II Sam. 5.2 and marginal references). The God who now returns at the head of his returning exiles is the same as he who once led his people out of Egypt 'with mighty hand and outstretched arm' (Deut. 4.34). We shall see, as the prophecy proceeds, that the return from Babylon is pictured as a second Exodus.

9. Zion . . . Jerusalem
Zion was properly the Jebusite city which David conquered (II Sam. 5.7) and was the south-east part of the later enlarged city. The two names are frequently in poetic parallelism.

that bringest good tidings
The LXX translates 'evangelist', thus preparing the way for the N.T. 'evangel' or good news. The RV 'O thou that tellest good tidings to Zion' would make Zion the recipient, not the bearer, of the evangel. It is a perfectly possible translation, but AV is to be preferred. Jerusalem has already heard the liberating word and is now to pass it on to her 'daughters'.

10. with strong hand
Better 'with strength' (LXX and DSI).

reward . . . work

Better 'reward . . . recompense' (RV). The word for WORK
is also used of the wages which are the recompense of toil
('wages' in Lev. 19.13). The thought is not that Yahweh is
to distribute largesse. His REWARD and 'recompense' are his
people, whom he has bought back by his labours for them.
The passage is reminiscent of Jer. 31.15f., where Rachel's
restored children are her reward for her long vigil of bitter
weeping.

11. The figure of the Good Shepherd, leading, not driving
his sheep, is frequent in the Bible: cf. Gen. 33.13f., where
Jacob says he must adjust his pace to that of the children, the
mother-ewes and their lambs, as here: cf. Ps. 23; Luke 15.3-7;
John 10.1-18.

the lambs עֲטָלִים

The Hebrew word became an epithet for a child, *talya* ('boy'),
talitha ('girl'). Jesus addressed the daughter of Jairus as
talitha (Mark 5.41). Every mother's child is a 'little lamb'.
One of the most beautiful of Blake's *Songs of Innocence* comes
to mind:

> *Little Lamb, who made thee?*
> *Dost thou know who made thee?*
> *Gave thee life, and bade thee feed*
> *By the stream and o'er the mead:*
> *Gave thee clothing of delight,*
> *Softest clothing, woolly, bright;*
> *Gave thee such a tender voice,*
> *Making all the vales rejoice?*
> *Little Lamb, who made thee?*
> *Dost thou know who made thee?*
>
> *Little lamb, I'll tell thee;*
> *Little lamb, I'll tell thee:*
> *He is callèd by thy name,*
> *For he calls himself a Lamb,*

> *He is meek, and He is mild,*
> *He became a little child.*
> *I a child, and thou a lamb,*
> *We are callèd by his name.*
> > *Little lamb, God bless thee!*
> > *Little lamb, God bless thee!*

THE INCOMPARABLE
40.12-26

Some scholars think that these verses are part of a single section
which extends to the end of the chapter, on the ground that
they are not in themselves a prophecy but only a preparation
for the exhortation to hope in vv. 27-31. Certainly they are
that in their present context, but they can quite well be taken
as a unit in themselves, a divine ' self-predication '. The whole
thought is for the moment centred upon Yahweh, not upon
man nor upon Israel's situation and need. The passage is in
form a monologue and the speaker is Yahweh himself (v. 25),
even though the references to him are otherwise in the third
person. Yahweh is the almighty and all-wise Creator (vv.
12-14), Lord of the nations (vv. 15-21) and of history (vv. 22-
24), and marshal of the hosts of heaven (vv. 25f.). The verses
are not a definition of pure monotheism but a description of
Yahweh as The Incomparable. The O.T. is not interested in
pure monotheism, simply as a doctrine. Yahweh is always
known for what he *is* by what he *does.*

It has been said recently that ' it can hardly be denied that
the cosmology of the ancient Hebrews is only the merest daub
compared with the sweeping grandeur of the picture revealed
by modern science' (Fred Hoyle, *The Nature of the Universe,*
p. 115). That is true enough, in its way. We can weigh the
earth and measure the universe in terms of millions of light-
years. DI only knew the two or three thousand stars that can
be seen with the naked eye, and they were nothing like so far
away for him as we know them to be. He knew nothing of the

countless millions of extra-galactic nebulae. Yet the majesty
of his description keeps pace with every expansion of the
expanding universe. No discoveries of the astro-physicist will
ever outdate this passage and Job 38, and it is safe to say that
no more magnificent poems on The Incomparable will ever be
written. Mr. Hoyle goes on to ask: 'Is it in any way reasonable to suppose that it was given to the Hebrews to understand
mysteries far deeper than anything I can comprehend, when it
is quite clear that they were completely ignorant of many
matters that seem commonplace to me?' His answer is No:
'that religion is but a blind attempt to find an escape from the
truly dreadful situation in which we find ourselves' (*loc. cit.*).
The true answer is more likely Yes: the prophecy does not
read like escapism, and even if DI was over-sanguine, it is
incredible that Jesus, with his 'Your heavenly Father
knoweth . . .' was an escapist.

12. This is a rhetorical question. It is disputed whether
the answer it expects is 'Yahweh', or 'no one'. The 'who'
of v. 13 certainly expects the second of these answers. The
thought is that no man can do the things that the questions
propose, let alone comprehend the Creator of all.

the span
The distance between the thumb and little finger of the outstretched hand.

a measure
The Hebrew denotes 'the third part' of some dry measure;
cf. our 'quart', a fourth part of a gallon.

scales . . . balance
Hebrew in the reverse order, the 'balance' being the beam
from which the scales hang.

13. Spirit of the LORD
SPIRIT should be spelt with a small *s* (as in RV). DI had not
in mind all that Christians associate with the Holy Spirit,

though what he says is true of the Holy Spirit of Christian belief. The passage is quoted in Rom. 11.34; I Cor. 2.16, where the English translation 'mind' adequately expresses the meaning here.

14. the path of judgment
The right or model path. 'Judgment' here has approximately the sense of law, whether in nature or in history. Notice the rhetorical piling up of clauses in this verse.

15. a drop of a bucket
That drips from a bucket when it is drawn up from a well.

the isles
The word includes the islands and coast-lands of the Mediterranean. The geographical horizons of the Hebrews did not extend beyond 'Tarshish', probably on the south-east coast of Spain.

16. The meaning is that if all the cedars of Lebanon were fuel for a sacrifice of all the wild animals upon it, even such a holocaust would be inadequate to do honour to Yahweh. The Prophet is not here concerned with the questions whether animal sacrifice has any religious value, or whether wild animals—as distinct from domesticated, cattle and sheep—are legal sacrificial offerings.

19f. A satirical description of idols and their manufacture. It is probable that 41.6f., which fits very loosely into its context, was originally a continuation of 40.19f. Together, the two passages make up one picture. It may even be that they originally had no connexion with 40.12-26, but were a fugitive piece which was split up into two fragments, which were then placed separately into what seemed appropriate contexts. Certainly, v. 22 would read less abruptly than it does if it were originally the continuation of v. 18; and v. 21, which is partly a duplication of v. 28, may have been 'stitched in', so to speak, to ease the transition from the inserted vv. 19f. to v. 22. The text at the end of v. 19 and the beginning of v. 20 is difficult

and may have suffered damage. The picture is of an image
made of a core of baser metal, or perhaps silver (cf. 30.22),
which is then overlaid with beaten gold. A poor man makes
do with a core of hard wood, which is cut to the required shape
by a CUNNING (i.e. 'skilful'—when the AV of the Bible was
made the word had not yet acquired its present sinister meaning) workman. Together they swink and sweat (41.6f.), and
encourage one another with ludicrous seriousness, all for the
purpose of making a 'god' which has to be fastened with
solder and nails, lest it should topple over! What a pitiable
likeness to the true God! (So in the present context, in which
vv. 19f. are the answer to the question in v. 18.) The passage
is elaborately satirical, but somehow it detracts from the
austere majesty of vv. 12-26. It is instructive to read it together
with 44.9-20 and Wisd. 13ff., which are elaborations of the
same theme.

22. Perhaps originally the continuation of v. 18, and to be
translated simply, 'That sitteth upon the circle of the earth'.
The reference is to the vault (cf. Prov. 8.27; Job 22.14 RV
marg.) or 'firmament' (Gen. 1.6f.), a dome-shaped cupola
over-arching the earth, into which the stars were studded and
whose function was to prevent the waters of the original chaos
from breaking through to deluge the ordered cosmos. Anyone
who has looked down from a skyscraper or an aeroplane can
have a faint glimmer of what the picture means, and the New
Cosmology only adds to its impressiveness.

as a curtain

Lit. 'as fine gauze' (cf. RV marg.). It hardly needs saying
that the Prophet knew nothing of the inter-stellar hydrogen,
though the words are entirely appropriate to it.

23f. princes

Potentates. Yahweh is Lord of history, the King of kings.
The age of the great Hebrew prophets was strewn with the
wreckage of empires and the rise and fall of military dictators,
many of them usurpers, 'strong men'. Their fate was in

Yahweh's hand. He had only to BLOW upon them and they wilted like grass (cf. v. 7) before the sirocco.

25. the Holy One
There is no article in the Heb.; HOLY ONE has ceased to be an attribute and become a proper name (see also Job. 6.10; Hab. 3.3).

26. The description is of the stars as the martial retinue of Yahweh (cf. Judg. 5.20). The thought is not the drowsy one that when darkness falls the stars ' peep out ' and that not one fails to shine. It is that Yahweh LEADS OUT their host BY NUMBER. When he calls ' By the right, number! ' they all number. NOT ONE FAILETH is, literally, ' not one lags behind '; the root from which the word comes is the same as that from which the word ' flock ' is formed, the ' laggard flock ' which the Good Shepherd gently leads.   רֶחְדָּל

Babylonia, where this prophecy originated, was the home and centre of star-worship. The Babylonian gods were mostly star-gods. Yet here is a prophet who makes bold to affirm that the God of his captive nation ' created ' the ' gods ' whom their captors worshipped. Never in all history has there been such a signal victory over defeat and humiliation. The word CREATED is the same as in Gen. 1.1. It does not in itself carry the meaning of creation out of nothing, but it is never used except with God as subject. It is worth noting that the New Cosmology is coming increasingly to speak of ' creation (out of nothing) ', though, paradoxically, some of those who speak of creation are chary of speaking of a CREATOR. Surely the logic of a creation which can—as it seems—be scientifically posited, is that there is a Creator, not that belief in the Creator is ' a blind attempt to find an escape '.

THE EAGLE WINGS OF FAITH
40.27-31

Even if these verses were not originally one with the preceding,
they make a magnificent climax to it. There are many who
can testify that their faith gains in poise and confidence the
more stupendous the creation is seen to be. There is something in the sublimity of the universe, with its amazing sym-
metry and precision, that steadies the nerves rather than racks
them with apprehension and uncertainty.

The nation is addressed by the name of the old ancestor
Jacob-Israel, whose relationship with God had been so
intimate. There is a note of reproach in the opening WHY?
Israel has fallen a prey to self-pity; he imagines that his WAY
is hidden from Yahweh and his JUDGMENT passed over un-
heeded by God. Does he not know, has he never heard, that
Yahweh is an everlasting God, the Creator of the ends of the
earth, who faints not, neither is weary? From this point the
passage rises upon eagle's pinions to a splendid crescendo,
until it touches earth once more in a diminuendo movement:
'they run and are not weary; they walk but do not faint'—a
perfect finale. It has sometimes been argued that these words
are an anticlimax, and some would delete them as a later
addition. 'On the contrary,' wrote Sir George Adam Smith,
in what has come to be a classic exposition of the passage, 'it
is a natural and a true climax, rising from the easier to the
more difficult, from the ideal to the real, from dream to duty,
from what can only be the rare occasions of life to what must
be life's usual and abiding experience. History followed this
course.' (*The Book of Isaiah*, 2nd ed., vol. II, p. 105.) Words-
worth's *Ode to Duty*, too, may be read as a commentary on the
verse:

> *Serene will be our days and bright,*
> *And happy will our nature be,*
> *When love is an unerring light,*

> *And joy its own security.*
> *And they a blissful course may hold*
> *Even now, who, not unwisely bold,*
> *Live in the spirit of this creed;*
> *Yet seek thy firm support, according to their need.*

27. My way
The word means almost 'destiny' or 'fate', similarly to Ps. 37.5; Jer. 10.23.

my judgment
My 'just right', not in the sense of recompense for innocence, but as over against the heathen, who have exceeded their commission to chastise Israel.

30. the young men shall utterly fall
'picked young warriors actually stumble'. The tenses in this and the following verse should probably be rendered as present, not future.

31. they shall mount up with wings as eagles
There may be a reference here to the popular belief that the eagle renews his pinions in his old age (cf. Ps. 103.5). This is not certain, though the translation 'they grow pinions like eagles' is perfectly possible.

II

ISAIAH 41

THE CONQUEROR FROM THE EAST
41.1-4

Jewish interpreters have generally referred this passage to Abraham's victory over the four kings (Gen. 14), and this opinion is shared by a few modern Christian commentators. The more general, and more likely, view is that it refers to the meteoric career of Cyrus (see Introduction, p. 14). The description agrees admirably with his early victories up to the fall of Sardis in the autumn of 547. The tenses in vv. 2-3 are present ('gives . . . makes . . . pursues . . . passes') as in RV, and the passage gives the impression that it was composed while the victories of Cyrus were still the subject of amazement and surprise. It is the earliest passage in the prophecy which can be dated with reasonable confidence. Cyrus, of course, had no aim but conquest, nor any consciousness of being 'raised up' by the God of an insignificant people of whom, up to that time, he may not even have heard. But the prophecy, which is put into the month of Yahweh himself, states, after the rhetorical questions of vv. 2 and 4, that it is Yahweh, 'the first and the last', who has called him, and, indeed, all 'the generations from the beginning'. When nations in antiquity suffered disaster, it was supposed to be due to the weakness of their gods and the superior might of the gods of their conquerors. Nothing in religious history is more astonishing than the way the Hebrew prophets asserted, as disaster threatened Israel, that it was Yahweh who even raised up heathen nations to chastise his own people (so Isa.

10.5-15, Assyria; Jer. 25.9, Nebuchadrezzar), and here, at the close of the exile, Cyrus to deliver them.

1. Keep silence before me
Lit. ' exhibit silence unto me '. The sentence is what is known in grammar as a 'pregnant' construction, one in which a verb which does not express motion is followed by a preposition which does. The full meaning is, ' Be silent and listen to what I have to say '. A permissible inference is that 'silent' prayer is not a merely passive attitude, but an active waiting upon God.

O islands
See 40.15, where 'isles' is the same word as here.

and let the people renew their strength
For PEOPLE read 'peoples' (RV). The words RENEW THEIR STRENGTH are natural in 40.31, where they describe the reward of those 'that wait upon the LORD '; they are not very appropriate here, in what is a peremptory summons to the nations to appear at the bar of judgement. It is probable that the text originally read ' and let the peoples draw near and come '; cf. the closing words of v. 5, which are metrically awkward where they stand, and may have been accidentally displaced from v. 1. We should then suppose that RENEW THEIR STRENGTH was repeated from 40.31 to fill the gap.

2. Who raised up the righteous man from the east, called him to his foot?
This translation would quite well fit Abraham. But a better translation is, ' Who has roused up from the east one whom victory meets wherever he goes? ' THE RIGHTEOUS *MAN* (AV) is definitely wrong; the word means 'righteousness' (as RV). Then 'righteousness' or 'right' comes, especially in DI, to stand for the 'success' or 'victory' by which a man secures his 'right'. For TO HIS FOOT cf. Gen. 30.30, where Jacob's words 'since my coming', or, more correctly, 'whithersoever I turned ' (RV), are, literally, ' at my foot '.

and made him rule over kings?
The verb can be vocalized to read 'and brings down kings
(in defeat)'. This is the reading of DSI.

3. even by a way that he had not gone with his feet
Lit. 'a path with his feet he does not tread', meaning that he
marches so swiftly that his feet scarcely touch the ground, like
the he-goat that 'touched not the ground' in Dan. 8.5.

(For vv. 6f. see on 40.19f. above.)

ISRAEL, THE CHOSEN SERVANT OF YAHWEH, HAS NOTHING TO FEAR
41.8-13

This passage, with its introductory BUT, has much the same
relation to vv. 1-4 as 40.27-31 has to 40.12-26. The doctrine
of the divine choice or election of Israel is deeply rooted in the
O.T. The book of Genesis is the story of how God, after the
Flood, gradually narrowed down the circle of his choice to
the descendants of Shem, 'the father of all the children of
Eber' (i.e. the Hebrews; Gen. 10.21; cf. 11.10,16), Terah
(11.27), Abraham, Isaac ('in Isaac shall thy seed be called',
not Ishmael, 21.12), and finally to Jacob and his descendants.
This interpretation of history is doubtless a simplification of
obscure and complicated tribal movements, but in the light of
its sequel, Christianity, and on a broad view of history, it is not
to be dismissed out of hand. In the passage before us, Yahweh
calls Abraham 'him whom I loved', and a very early passage
in Genesis (15.18) speaks of his making a 'covenant' with
Abraham. The word SERVANT means literally 'slave', but it
was very far from being a term of reproach or disparagement.
It expressed the weaker partner's relation to the stronger in a
covenant. As such the SERVANT was a privileged person, and
was entitled, as of right, to look to his master for protection
and even love. Naturally he, for his part, was expected to be
obedient; he was called to service, more than to privilege.

Under the stress of exile the Jews might well conclude that Yahweh had finally cast them away, as he had every right to do, for their unfaithfulness to their part of the covenant. The Prophet of the exile reassures them, in Yahweh's name, saying in effect that Yahweh would never forsake the seed of the man whom he had loved through long and toilsome journeyings in the hallowed past.

10. be not dismayed
Lit. ' do not look around (in apprehension and fear)'.

with the right hand of my righteousness
Or, 'with my victorious right hand' (cf. v. 2 above).

11-12. incensed against . . . strive with . . . contended
(better RV **contend**) **with . . . war against.** These words describe the mounting violence of Israel's enemies; they may be rendered 'are angry with . . . go to law with . . . use physical force against . . . and (finally) declare open war'. But their fury can avail nothing, since Yahweh holds the right hand of his servant.

THE FEEBLE WORM SHALL BECOME A THRESHING-SLEDGE
41.14-16

This passage, with its opening FEAR NOT, is closely related, on the 'domino' principle (see above, p. 21), to the preceding paragraph (cf. v. 10); but here Israel is addressed as feminine, not masculine, and the figures employed, WORM and THRESH-ING-SLEDGE, are different. No contrast could be more striking than that between the humiliation and dejection of Israel as she is, and what Yahweh purposes to make her. It is even more striking in the Hebrew than in English, since it would appear that the word translated YE MEN OF actually meant 'louse'! The modern Christian bridles up at any suggestion

that he is a WORM, and he dislikes hymns which require him
so to call himself. But when Thomas Olivers wrote:

> *He calls a worm his friend,*
> *He calls himself my God,*

he was making the salvation of God the more wonderful by
contrast with what he had been saved from and what he
deserved, exactly as the Prophet does here. The threshing-
sledge was a heavy wooden board studded with metal teeth on
its under-side (cf. Amos 1.3). After it had been dragged round
the threshing-floor, the mixed grain and chaff were tossed into
the air and the chaff was carried away by the wind. The
threshing-sledge that Israel is to become will be *new* and *many-
toothed* (so the Hebrew implies), and it will be as powerful as
modern machines and explosives.

14. thy redeemer
The conception of Yahweh as Israel's redeemer is more
prominent in DI (some fifteen times) than anywhere else in
the O.T. We must of course be careful not to read back into
it all the associations it has acquired in Christian theology.
Even so, it has a rich content and it cannot be translated by
any one word. The noun REDEEMER (Hebrew *gō'ēl*) is the
participle of a verb (*gā'al*). Among the English words by
which it is rendered are 'kinsman' or 'near kinsman' (so
nine times in Ruth), 'avenger (of blood)' (Num. 35.12; Deut.
19.6,12; Josh. 20.3,5,9) and 'revenger' (six times in AV of
Num. 35.19-27; RV 'avenger'). The verb is used in Lev.
25.25f.,48f. of a man's 'redeeming' the estate of a relative who
has fallen into poverty, or the relative himself if he has had
to sell himself into slavery to get out of debt. These usages
indicate that a *gō'ēl* was the kinsman upon whom devolved
the duty of caring for the interests of his relative by every
means in his power, whether by 'redeeming' him or his
property during his lifetime, or avenging his death if he had
been murdered. So close are the ties that bind Israel to her

REDEEMER, and the Holy One of Israel (twice in this passage) will never repudiate his voluntarily imposed obligations.

THE DESERT SHALL BECOME AN OASIS
41.17-20

This theme is developed more fully in chaps. 35; 43.18-21; 49.9-11. It has already been anticipated in 40.10f., and there are echoes of it in 48.21; 55.13. The paragraph begins abruptly and pictures the exiles as though they have already set out on the journey home. It reads as if the Prophet is anticipating objections about the difficulties and hardships of the journey. The poor and needy will seek for water and find none, and their tongues will be parched with thirst. In that event, comes the divine answer, ' I, YAHWEH, WILL ANSWER THEM; I, THE GOD OF ISRAEL, WILL NOT FORSAKE THEM '—always this emphasis upon the indissoluble bond between Yahweh and his people. Long ago, on the journey from Egypt to Canaan, he had miraculously brought water out of the rock (48.21; Ex. 17.1-7; Num. 20.1-13). He will do no less during this second Exodus. Indeed, he will do more: he will open rivers on the treeless heights (RV ' on the bare heights ' is better than AV IN HIGH PLACES), and springs in the valleys. The desert highway will become a permanent oasis in which forest trees will grow. What some of these trees were is obscure, partly because in our northern clime we have no species exactly corresponding to them: SHITTAH should be ' acacia ' (RV), OIL TREE some kind of wild olive or ' oleaster ' (RV marg.), PINE may be ' elm ' or ' plane ' (RV marg.), and BOX TREE ' cypress ' (RV marg.). Notice the word TOGETHER at the end of the list of trees, and again in v. 20 after the verbs SEE . . . KNOW . . . CONSIDER . . . AND UNDERSTAND. DI is fond of it as a means of binding together what are practically synonyms and it is a good example of his voluminous and rhetorical style.

THE PROOF OF YAHWEH'S SOLE DEITY IS THAT HE ALONE FOREKNOWS THE FUTURE AND HAS DETERMINED THE CAREER OF CYRUS
41.21-29

This section is in two related parts, vv. 21-24 and 25-29 (cf. the two paragraphs in RV). The first asserts as a general principle that Yahweh alone among the gods can predict the future; the second asserts, as an actual example, that it is he who raised up Cyrus. The inference is that he knows the future because he, in fact, determines it. The heathen gods are dumb and helpless nothings.

Verses 21-24 picture a divine assize, in which the credentials of the gods are to be examined and judged. There has already been an anticipation of this in 41.1, where the peoples were summoned to the bar of judgment. Now it is the turn of their gods. The word CAUSE in v. 21 means a suit at law, and the verse may be translated, 'Present your case, says Yahweh; advance your arguments, says the King of Jacob'. Then, in v. 22, 'Let them (the gods) come forward (so the major versions) and tell us what is going to happen'. What THE FORMER THINGS are has occasioned much discussion. They probably refer, not to happenings in the distant past, but to those already described in 41.2f., the early victories of Cyrus, of which Yahweh had, through the Prophet, announced the significance while as yet they were contemporary. Did any other god discern their import? Does any even now understand their significance (WHAT THEY BE) that we may know what still to expect from them? Or, if the gods are silent about the past, let them announce things that lie yet in the future, that we may know what shall be the issue of them—inverting the order of the clauses AND KNOW (lit. 'that we may know') THE LATTER END OF THEM and OR DECLARE US THINGS FOR TO COME, which gives a better sense and is also better poetry. Indeed, let the gods do anything at all, either good or bad!

Only let them show some signs of life and animation! The conclusion of the disputation is, ' See! you are less (marg. " worse ") than nothing, and your work less than nought; to choose you is to choose what is loathsome! '

Herodotus relates that when Croesus of Lydia was faced with the prospect of having to measure his power with that of Cyrus, he took the initiative and himself prepared to attack Media, which had recently been absorbed by Persia. He was immensely rich—' rich as Croesus ' has become proverbial— and sent lavish gifts to all the famous oracles of Greece and even beyond, praying them to let him know what would be the outcome of the campaign. ' We can understand that for all this Croesus got the best advice consistent with the ignorance and caution of the priests whom he consulted. The oracles told him that if he went against Cyrus he would destroy a great empire; but he forgot to ask, whether it was his own or his rival's ' (Sir George Adam Smith, *The Book of Isaiah*, vol. II, 2nd ed., 1927, p. 117). The oracles of the gods always took care to be on the right side, on the principle, ' Heads I win, tails you lose! ' The story which Herodotus tells is the most illuminating commentary on this passage. The Prophet had every reason to be satirical about idols. Even if he had not heard of Croesus' consultation of the Greek oracles, the oracles of the Babylonian gods did not inspire any more confidence than they (cf. 47.13f.).

In vv. 25-29 Yahweh states explicitly what he had already implied in the rhetorical question of 41.2, namely that it was he who raised up Cyrus. The translation RAISED UP hardly does justice to the vigour of the Hebrew, which means ' roused up ', ' stirred up to activity '. The emphasis of the passage is not upon what Cyrus is still going to do, but upon what he had already done: ' I roused up one from the north, and he *came*.' His empire, now incorporating Media and Lydia, extended in a great arc from the east of Babylonia round to the Aegean. He could thus be said to come both from the north and east; indeed, if Hebrew wanted to say ' north-east ', it would have to name both points of the compass in parallelism, as here.

That Cyrus is to invoke Yahweh (CALL UPON MY NAME) is a
bold assertion, and some would emend the text to 'one whom
I (Yahweh) call by name', as in 45.3. This is hazardous, and,
even in the light of 45.3 ('that thou mayest know that I am
Yahweh'), is unnecessary. For monotheistic faith all active
enterprise is service of the one God, even though the human
instrument is not fully conscious of the significance of what
he is doing (cf. Mal. 1.11 (RV); Jer. 25.9). By a change of
vowel points—which were not part of the original text—a
change which gives a more natural construction, v. 25 continues in the past tense, AND HE CAME UPON PRINCES AS UPON
MORTAR. The insertion of a single consonant, which has
probably fallen out because it is the same as the first letter
of the next word, would give a more forcible simile: 'and
he trampled princes like mortar (or mire).' The word translated PRINCES is a loan-word from Babylonian, and means
prefects of provinces.

26. He is righteous
Better, 'It is right!'

27. The first SHALL SAY to Zion, Behold, behold them
Lit. 'First to Zion, Behold, behold them', which is not very
intelligible. There is reason to believe that the word rendered
FIRST could mean something like 'leading counsel', and for
BEHOLD, BEHOLD THEM LXX has 'I give'. That would make
a verse with perfect parallelism: 'I appoint leading counsel for
Zion, and give to Jerusalem a bearer of good tidings (of
acquittal).'
   28. Lit. 'And I look, and there is no man, and of these and
there is no counsellor, who, if I asked them, could answer a
word.' The first half of this gives no clear sense. Who are
'these'? The LXX appears to have read something like,
'And of the nations, behold there is none, and of their idols
(gods) there is no counsellor——' This would give an excellent sense in the context, and the word 'of these' may well be
a corruption of 'their gods'.

29. confusion

Emptiness, nothingness (cf. 44.9, 'vanity', RV marg. 'confusion'). It is the word translated 'waste' (Gen. 1.2 RV) in description of the primeval chaos.

III

ISAIAH 42

THE SERVANT OF YAHWEH: HIS
ENDOWMENT AND MISSION
42.1-4

This is the first of four passages generally known as the 'Songs of the Servant'. The other three are 49.1-6; 50.4-9; 52.13-53.12. The question, 'Who was the Servant of the Songs?' has been more widely discussed, and has received a greater variety of answers, than any other single O.T. problem. In DI outside the Songs Israel is several times called the servant of Yahweh (41.8f.; 44.1f.,21; 45.4; 48.20). Within the Songs the Servant is anonymous, except in 49.3, and there in a sense which obviously needs qualification (see note on the passage). The character of the Servant in the Songs is also different from that of Israel in the main prophecy, so that we cannot take it for granted that he is Israel here. The view that he is Israel has been, and still is, widely held. All that we need note at the moment is that elsewhere in the O.T. the term 'servant' of Yahweh is applied to individuals; examples are II Sam. 3.18 (David); Ezek. 34.23f. (the Messianic David); Hag. 2.23 (Zerubbabel); Jer. 27.6 (Nebuchadrezzar) and Amos 3.7 (of the prophets).

The speaker in the passage is Yahweh. Who the audience are is not stated. They can hardly be the Gentiles, who are referred to in the third person. They are perhaps heavenly beings. The Servant is introduced as already present, but his mission and its fulfilment are still in the future.

1. Yahweh calls the Servant MY SERVANT . . . MY CHOSEN

(RV), exactly the words used of Israel in 41.8; 44.1f.; 45.4.
The expression MY (thy, his, etc.) SOUL is often a paraphrase
for the personal pronoun I (thou, he, etc.), especially in poetry;
the meaning is, therefore, ' my chosen in whom I delight '. It
is generally agreed that the words which Jesus heard at his
baptism, 'Thou art my beloved Son, in whom I am well
pleased' (Mark 1.11) are a conflation of two O.T. passages,
' Thou art my son ' (Ps. 2.7) and this in the first Servant Song.
This would mean that at his baptism Jesus was conscious of
combining in his own person the vocations of the promised
Messiah and the Suffering Servant.

The Servant is endowed with Yahweh's spirit. What this
implies may be inferred from Isa. 11.2, where the spirit of
Yahweh is defined as ' the spirit of wisdom and understanding,
the spirit of counsel and might, the spirit of knowledge and of
the fear of Yahweh '. He is to BRING FORTH JUDGMENT TO THE
GENTILES, i.e. the non-Jewish nations, or, as we should say, the
heathen. JUDGMENT is used in a wide sense of the sum-total
of the ordinances of the religion of Yahweh, similarly to
II Kings 17.26f., where the word (*mishpāt*) is rendered
' manner ', and Jer. 5.4f. It is almost equivalent to ' the true
religion '. HE SHALL BRING FORTH is literally ' he shall cause
to go forth (from his mouth)', i.e. announce. This may be
elucidated from Jer. 15.19, where the meaning is, ' if you speak
what is precious, unmixed with what is cheap and worthless,
you shall be as my mouth '.

2. The Servant will not make any clamour. The contrast
may be with the early ecstatic prophets, who worked themselves up into frenzied excitement by artificial means such as
music and dancing; or it may be with denunciatory prophets
like Amos; or again it may be with conquerors like Cyrus.
It is widely held that the Servant is intended as a foil to
Cyrus.

3. This verse is a fine example of the figure of speech
known as litotes, in which an affirmation is made indirectly by
the negation of its contrary, as when St. Paul called himself
' a citizen of no mean city ', meaning that he was a citizen of

a very illustrious city (Acts 21.39). Isaac Watts caught the
spirit of the verse perfectly when he wrote:

> *He'll never quench the smoking flax,*
> *But raise it to a flame:*

Or, to quote another line from the same hymn, the Servant is
'touched with a sympathy within'.

smoking flax
Dimly burning wick (as RV marg.).

unto truth
Better 'in truth' (RV) or 'faithfully'.
   4. The Servant shall not fail (RV marg. 'burn dimly'), nor
himself be discouraged (RV marg. 'bruised', repeating the
figures of v. 3 and applying them to the Servant), until he has
established true religion in the earth, and for his instruction the
far coastlands wait with eager expectation.

> *Far and wide, though all unknowing,*
> *Pants for Thee each mortal breast.*

his law
The primary meaning of the Hebrew word for LAW (*torah*) is
'instruction', and the narrower sense of law or commandment
is derived from this. Here it means teaching or instruction
rather than 'the Law' as embodied in the Pentateuch.
   There is sharp difference of opinion on the question whether
the Servant is depicted as a king or as a prophet. Most
features in the description could apply to both, though, so
far as we know, *torah* was never given by a king, but either
by priests or prophets. On the whole, the Servant looks more
like a prophet than a king, but it is likely that he combines
something of the functions of both and is not to be placed in
either category to the exclusion of the other. There have been
scholars who have thought that the Servant in this passage is
Cyrus.

THE CALL OF THE SERVANT
42.5-9

Some scholars think that these verses are so inseparable from the preceding that the whole paragraph should be treated as a unit. Accordingly they would make the first Song consist of vv. 1-9. Against this it may be argued that the introductory words THUS SAITH GOD THE LORD indicate a new beginning, and also that the person addressed (THEE v. 6) is different from the audience addressed in vv. 1-4. Of those who treat vv. 5-9 separately, some think that the address is to Cyrus, others that it is to the Servant. Of the latter, some think that the Servant is Israel, others that he is an individual Servant distinct from Israel. This last group generally regard vv. 5-9 as a second Servant Song. The difficulties of the passage are considerable, and a detailed discussion of them, besides taking up too much space, might only confuse the reader. (For a detailed discussion see my *The Suffering Servant in Deutero-Isaiah*, pp. 131-5.)

The view taken here is that in its original form the passage was addressed to Israel, and that the second half of v. 6 (from AND WILL KEEP THEE) was later inserted to make it apply to an individual Servant, thus transforming it into a 'secondary' Servant Song. Originally, the subject of v. 7 was Yahweh, who was to deliver Israel from the physical hardships of the exile; in its present form the Servant is to deliver the Gentiles from their spiritual blindness.

5. God the LORD
Lit. 'the (true) God, Yahweh'.

that created the heavens, and stretched them forth
See on 40.22,26.

that spread forth the earth
Lit. 'that beat out the earth'. The verb is related to the

noun 'firmament' (Gen. 1.6), which was pictured as beaten out (of metal). The cosmology of DI has many similarities to that of Gen. 1.

that which cometh out of it
The Hebrew conveys the idea of teeming or abundant life.

breath . . . spirit
These words are in parallelism. The primary meaning of SPIRIT (*ruach*) is wind, air in motion. As attributed to God, in the expression 'the spirit of God (or Yahweh)', it denotes his invincible, dynamic energy (cf. Judg. 6.34 and marginal references). God *is* spirit (cf. Isa. 31.3). According to the early creation story man became a living soul (or entity) when Yahweh 'breathed into his nostrils the breath (*neshamah*) of life' (Gen. 2.7). Also, in quite early times, man was thought to possess 'spirit' (Gen. 45.27; Judg. 15.19), though this 'spirit' is not directly related to God. During and after the exile man came to be thought of as endowed with spirit bestowed upon him directly by God (Ezek. 11.19f.; 36.26), thus becoming related to God on the higher side of his nature. In Ps. 104.29f. even the animals are said to possess *ruach* ('breath' in v. 29 is properly 'spirit', as in v. 30). Similarly here, THEM THAT WALK THEREIN may include all living creatures.

6. keep
'form' (RV marg.) is an equally possible translation, and this sense is more usual in DI. The idea may be derived from Jer. 1.5 (cf. Isa. 44.2,24; 49.5).

a covenant of the people
A medium through whom Yahweh is to make a (new) covenant with Israel (cf. 49.5,8).

a light of the Gentiles
cf. 49.6. The mission of the servant is to be both to Israel and

to the heathen, as in 49.5f. Both missions are fulfilled in
Jesus (Luke 2.32).

9. the former things
See on 41.21-29.

THE NEW SONG
42.10-17

This passage consists of (1) an introductory summons to
praise (vv. 10-12), (2) graphic descriptions of Yahweh under
the figures of a warrior and a woman in travail (vv. 13-15),
leading up to (3) the now familiar theme of the exodus from
Babylon (vv. 16f.). It should be compared with Ps. 33.3-22;
96; 98; and 149, which similarly begin with an exordium to
SING UNTO YAHWEH A NEW SONG. If the psalms are read care-
fully it will be seen that they conform more or less to a
common pattern, generally known as a community thanks-
giving: following (1) the summons to praise, there is (2) a
glorification of Yahweh either as world-creator and/or victor
over the nations and/or their gods, and finally (3) an announce-
ment of his coming to judge the world. There are striking
verbal similarities between the Psalms and DI. Clearly there
is literary relationship between them. Whether the pattern
was created by DI and then adopted by the psalmists, or vice
versa, is a subject of keen discussion, but the opinion is gaining
ground that it was the Prophet who made use of a well-estab-
lished psalm-type. Either way, a comparison of the New Song
in DI with the psalms named makes two things clear: (1) that
the violent similes in vv. 13-15 are not so incongruous in their
context as at first sight they appear, and (2) that if the concluding verses relating to the exodus from Babylon correspond
to the psalmist's picture of Yahweh coming to judge the world,
it must be assumed that the Prophet thought of the return of
the exiles as the triumphant culmination of Yahweh's purpose.
In other words, the passage is eschatological; it has to do with

what DI expected would be *the last things*. A new world will
be born of the divine travail. It may be noted that the expression A NEW SONG has an eschatological ring in Rev. 5.9.

10-12. The summons to praise is addressed to THE END OF
THE EARTH, that is to the most distant peoples known to the
Prophet. These are included under two main groups, the
coastlands (ISLES) of the west (see on 40.15) and the encamp-
ments (VILLAGES) of the Arabian steppe-dwellers in the east.
The words THEIR VOICE (v. 11) are not in the Hebrew, but are
supplied by the translators as the object of the transitive verb
LIFT UP. A slight change in the Hebrew, which has some support in the ancient versions, would give a translation, 'Let
the wilderness and its cities exult'. Kedar (cf. 21.16; 60.7;
Jer. 49.28) is typical of the nomad Bedouin tribes, and in Jer.
2.10 is in parallelism with THE ISLES, to denote 'east and west',
as here. For THE ROCK RV has Sela (the modern Petra); but
since it is parallel with THE TOP OF THE MOUNTAINS the AV
should probably stand.

13. Translate, 'Yahweh shall go forth as a warrior, like a
man of war he shall stir up zeal; he shall utter a war-cry, he
shall roar aloud, against his enemies he shall show himself
a mighty one.'

14. The figure changes to that of a woman in travail.
Translate: 'Far too long have I held my peace, keeping silence
and restraining myself; like a woman in child-birth will I groan,
I will gasp and pant together.'

15. Describes the effect of these (on the surface) incongruous similes: mountains and hills will be devastated,
rivers turned to desert wastes, and standing pools dried up
—the exact opposite of the desert transformed into an oasis
of 41.18f.

These similes strike the western reader as extremely violent,
even objectionable, notwithstanding that the divine zeal is
kindled by compassion for the helpless and enslaved. The
figure of the warrior-God goes back to the Exodus (Ex. 15.3),
when Yahweh delivered his people from Egypt. An even more
violent picture is that of the blood-stained warrior of Isa.

63.1-6. The language of these passages is not merely anthropomorphic, it is anthropopathic; that is to say, it ascribes to God not only a human form (Greek *anthropos*, ' man '+ *morphé*, ' form '), but even human feelings and passions (Greek *pathein*, ' to suffer '; cf. our words ' pathos ' and ' sympathy '). Our instinct is to say that such passages ought to have no place in Holy Scripture. But before we say that, we shall do well to look at the sequel. It was natural for the Hebrews to assume that if and when God visited the earth in judgment, there would be carnage; blood would be shed. When he did come in the Incarnation, blood was shed; but it was man, not God, that shed it, and the blood that was shed was not that of man, but the blood of the incarnate Son of God. One of two things may happen to an anthropomorphic and anthropopathic conception of God : it may either be outgrown and give place to an abstract and coldly transcendent conception; or, if it is retained, it will, quite logically, find its culmination in a doctrine of Incarnation. That is what happened. The Hebrews firmly believed that God is personal, active in history, and since they were convinced of that they could never think of him as indifferent to the fate of the world. He would *act*— that is the permanent significance of the violent similes in this paragraph. He *did* act, but the way in which he acted was very different from what was anticipated of him. ' God sent not his Son into the world to condemn the world; but that the world through him might be saved ' (John 3.17).

16. These things will I do unto them, and not forsake them
Better, ' These are the things I will do, and I will not leave them undone.'

THE DEAF AND BLIND SERVANT
42.18-25

This passage lacks something of the clarity and brilliance so generally characteristic of DI. Its language is inferior and rather 'ragged', and the text is sometimes obscure. Note, for example, the change of pronouns, THOU . . . HE, in v. 20. This does not necessarily mean that it is not from DI, but, if it is from him, it looks as if it has been expanded in the circle of his disciples. We not infrequently find in the prophetical books passages which have not the sure touch of the master, and it would appear that to his authentic utterances there were gathered words from anonymous sources, and that the disciples sometimes modified the originals or themselves composed passages which they felt to be in the spirit of the master. It may be remarked that there are not many such passages in DI. Where they are found it is helpful to think of them as in some sort the earliest commentaries on the prophets, and the fact that they are bound up with the words of the masters should make us treat with respect these utterances of the 'secondarily inspired'. Evidently, men of lesser inspiration felt that they also had a word of the Lord to declare. From this the preacher and teacher to-day may take courage.

The blind and deaf servant is obviously Israel, and the verses probably owe their place here to the catchword BLIND, which relates them to the preceding paragraph. The Prophet, or whoever was the author, is perfectly frank about the moral and spiritual blindness of his people. The fact that they are portrayed in such an unfavourable light is not, in itself, sufficient reason for denying the passage to DI, who had no illusions about his people (cf. 43.22-28). The main emphasis in the paragraph is that it was Yahweh who brought upon his people the disaster of the exile, in order to discipline them to obedience, and not, as some of them might be only too ready to argue, the Babylonians. When we look at the history of the Israelite kingdoms, it is only natural for us to assume that it was inevitable that they would be swallowed up by the empires of Assyria and Babylon. The prophets always insisted that their fall was due to their disobedience to Yahweh, that it was a divine judgement, and not simply a political misfortune due to the fact that they were weak and their enemies strong.

19. perfect

Hebrew *meshullam*. The meaning is wholly dubious and the text uncertain. The best translation we can give to the word as it stands is something like 'in a covenant of peace (with me)', cf. RV, or 'devoted (to God)'. A change of vowels to *moshlam* would give a sense similar to that of the Arabic word *muslim*, of which the literal meaning is 'one who is submissive (to God)'. *Meshullam* has been taken as a proper name, that of the servant of Yahweh (see p. 31). This is very dubious.

21. the law

The Hebrew has LAW simply, without the article. The emphasis is not here upon the legal portions of the Pentateuch, but upon 'teaching' (so RV marg.) or 'instruction' generally (see on 42.4). The same applies to LAW in v. 24, where also the RV marg. has 'teaching'.

IV

ISAIAH 43

NOTHING CAN HARM, FOR GOD IS THERE
43.1-7

1. This passage begins with BUT NOW, as if to relate it to what precedes. (That being so we may assume that the nucleus of the preceding paragraph is by DI.) The hopeless situation in which the exiles now find themselves is to be followed by a future rich in promise. We expect the Prophet to say, 'Rejoice!' Instead, remembering their despondency, he says, FEAR NOT! (repeated in v. 5, cf. 41.10,13f.; 44.2; 54.4—the words run like a thread through the prophecy). Yahweh is he who CREATED Jacob and FORMED Israel. The thought of Yahweh as creator has already appeared in the prophecy; here it is applied particularly to Israel. The creator of the world and its peoples (42.5) is in a peculiar sense the creator of Israel. For FORMED with reference to Israel see 43.21; 44.2,21,24, etc.

The early Hebrews assumed the existence of other gods besides Yahweh (cf. Judg. 11.24; I Sam. 26.19), though they recognized that it would be wrong for them to worship any god but their own. The world was supposed to be divided up into areas, each ruled over by its own god, who was entitled to the worship of the people within his own territory. It is one of the paradoxes of O.T. religion that when the Hebrews came to believe in one only God, they continued to think of him as having a special interest in themselves. At first sight monotheism seems inconsistent with any doctrine of election. Yet

when we view the whole course of Hebrew history, together
with its sequel, Christianity, it does seem evident that the
Hebrews' faith in their election was not just a naïve survival
of a primitive fancy (cf. on 41.8-13). God did choose Israel,
not to privilege indeed, but for service. Such is the teaching
of the Bible, and it is entirely credible. Christ was a Jew, and
he would have been unintelligible if he had appeared anywhere
else in the world, and without the long period of training in
the knowledge of God to which the Jews had to submit themselves. What the world knows of God is due in large measure
to what Israel believed, and suffered.

For Yahweh as Israel's Redeemer see on 41.14. The past
tense (I HAVE REDEEMED THEE) denotes, in Hebrew idiom, that
the promised redemption is certain, as good as already accomplished. That Israel is called by Yahweh's name is the token
that she belongs to him as his intimate possession—THOU ART
MINE (cf. II Sam. 12.28; Amos 9.12).

2. Whatever perils may threaten his people, Yahweh will
be with them. Fire and water are mentioned together in
Ps. 66.12 as embracing all extremes of hideous danger. The
reference here is not to dangers attending the homeward
journey to Palestine—these are to be overcome by supernatural
means, cf. 41.18-20—but in general to the dangers that
threaten God's people anywhere. It is probable that the story
of Shadrach, Meshach, and Abednego in the burning fiery
furnace (Dan. 3) is a development from this motif of passing
unscathed through fire.

3. For THE HOLY ONE OF ISRAEL see Introduction, p. 18,
and on 41.14. The word SAVIOUR with the possessive pronoun
occurs in 49.26, and alone in 43.11; 45.15,21. It is almost a
proper name and the AV is hardly reading too much into the
word when it spells it with a capital S. (The reader will do
well to trace the word, together with the verb 'save', through
the O.T. with the aid of a concordance.) It has a wide content. What it implies in this context is explained in what
follows: Yahweh does not hesitate to give the rich lands of
Africa as the price of his people's ransom. Seba is to be dis-

tinguished from Sheba, on the Arabian side of the Red Sea;
it denotes properly the country south of Ethiopia (Hebrew
Cush). Cush and Seba correspond roughly to what we call
Upper Egypt and the Sudan. Together with Egypt proper they
were all of Africa known to the world in O.T. times. It has
sometimes been suggested that the text means that Yahweh
will give the African territories to Cyrus in return for his
liberation of the Jews. This should not be pressed. The
'ransom' metaphor has sometimes been applied too rigorously,
as in the early Church, when it was supposed that Christ paid
the ransom price of man to the Devil! Moreover, it was not
until the time of Cambyses, the successor of Cyrus, that Egypt
was conquered by Persia. The word GAVE should be translated 'give' or 'will give'; there is no reference here to the
earlier Exodus from Egypt.

4. The ransom figure is continued, Yahweh's motive being
stated as his love for Israel (cf. Deut. 7.8; Hos. 11.1; 14.4; Jer.
31.20); translate 'Because thou art precious . . . honourable,
and I love thee' (present tenses). For MEN (*adam*) read probably 'lands' (*adamoth*). PEOPLE should be 'peoples' (RV).

5-7. After a repeated FEAR NOT, Yahweh is depicted as
bringing the exiles back from the four points of the compass.
Already in the sixth century the Jews were widely scattered.
Some had gone down to Egypt (Jer. 43) and it is known that
there was a colony at Elephantine, near the first Cataract
(see on 49.12). The northern tribes had been deported to
Assyria. Jeremiah (Jer. 31.1-22) and Ezekiel (Ezek. 37.15-28)
looked for a reunion of all the sons of Israel under a ruler of
the house of David. They thought, not of two kingdoms,
Israel and Judah, but of *one* people of God, and when DI
speaks of Israel and Jacob in parallelism, as he frequently does,
it is this one people that he has in mind. He did not concern
himself with the question whether Palestine could support them
all (see on 49.14-21); what he was concerned with was the idea
of the unity of the people of God.

YAHWEH ALONE IS GOD AND ISRAEL
IS HIS WITNESS
43.8-13

The situation here is forensic, similar to that in 41.1-4 and
41.21-24, but with a new element, viz. that Yahweh's people
are summoned as his witnesses in his controversy with the
heathen gods and their devotees. They look unpromising witnesses enough, blind and deaf (v. 8, cf. 42.18ff.). There are
three parties in the dispute, the nations (v. 9), the Israelites
(v. 10), and finally Yahweh (vv. 11-13). The court sits; ALL
THE NATIONS ARE GATHERED TOGETHER (this is the most natural
translation of the opening words of v. 9). Can any of them
point to evidences that they or their gods ever knew anything
of the course history would take? It is possible that WHO and
THEM refer obliquely to the gods, who are challenged to pro-
duce witnesses from among their own worshippers, if they can.
Presumably no witnesses are forthcoming. Then Yahweh turns
to his own people—YOU ARE MY WITNESSES, IT IS THE VERY
WORD OF YAHWEH. It is a humble enough service that his
people render him, nothing like so all-embracing, in this context, as a world-wide mission; and a large part of its purpose
is to strengthen the faith of the Israelites themselves—THAT
YOU MAY KNOW AND BELIEVE ME, AND UNDERSTAND THAT I AM
HE. I AM HE, is the monotheistic formula (cf. 41.4). In the
heathen world, gods were born and even died. There were
fashions in gods and one god might supplant another as an
object of devotion. When Yahweh says that before him no
god was FORMED, as though he himself had been formed, the
word is ironical. He, and he alone, always was God, and
always will be. The magnificent self-predication continues in
vv. 11-13. Notice the cumulative force of the repetition 'I
("even" is not in the Hebrew), I', and the climactic verbs
DECLARED . . . SAVED . . . SHEWED.

13. before the day was

The Hebrew is obscure. LXX and some other versions read
'from eternity'. A slight textual change would give 'this
(very) day'.

who shall let it

LET in the old meaning of 'hinder'; cf. 'without let or
hindrance'. The Hebrew means 'turn back', 'reverse';
nothing can stand in Yahweh's way.

BABYLON'S FALL
43.14-15

In this short oracle, which may be only a fragment, Babylon
is named for the first time in the prophecy. The framework
(vv. 14a,15) is in what are by now familiar terms. For Yahweh
as the King of Israel cf. 41.21; 44.6. The text of 14b is obscure
and probably corrupt. The versions evidently did not understand it and any attempt to reconstruct it is largely guesswork.
The Hebrew may be rendered literally: 'For your sake I (will)
send to Babylon, and will bring down (as) fugitives all of
them, and the Chaldeans in the ships of their ringing cry' (cf.
RV). For 'fugitives' cf. 46.1-2, where the Babylonian gods
are depicted as being carried into safety on the backs of pack-
animals. Of 'the ships of their ringing cry' two interpretations have been offered: (1) the ships in which they pride
themselves (cf. RV), (2) with reference to the boat-songs by
which the rowers timed their rowing. 'Chaldeans' is a
synonym for Babylonians. The Chaldeans were a Semitic
people who settled in the lower Euphrates valley and after a
long struggle wrested Babylon from the Assyrians, by whom it
had been conquered, and established the Chaldean or 'neo-
Babylonian' empire after the fall of Nineveh in 612 B.C.
Notice that Yahweh does not say he will send *Cyrus* to
Babylon, though that is what he will do. But like everything
else in DI this oracle is theocentric; Yahweh is all.

THE NEW AND MORE WONDERFUL
EXODUS
43.16-21

The homeward journey through the transformed desert has
already been described in 41.17-20, but without explicitly com-
paring and contrasting it with the first Exodus from Egypt.
Here that contrast is intentionally drawn. The tenses in
vv. 16f. are past: THUS SAITH YAHWEH, WHO MADE A WAY
. . . WHO LED FORTH CHARIOT AND HORSE (the nouns are col-
lectives) . . . THEY LAY DOWN, THEY DID NOT ARISE; THEY
WERE EXTINGUISHED, THEY WERE QUENCHED LIKE A WICK.
The reference is clearly to Yahweh's first deliverance from the
slavery of Egypt. But even it shall pale before the NEW
THING which Yahweh is about to do, making a pathway in the
wilderness and rivers in the howling waste. The very denizens
of the waste will honour Yahweh for this wondrous change in
their habitat. (We must not expect the Prophet to reflect that,
being the creatures they are, they would probably set out to
find another desert!).

20. the beast of the field
Wild creatures (collective, cf. RV).

dragons
Hebrew *tannim*, usually understood as ' jackals ' (RV), howling
in waste places (cf. 34.13; Mic. 1.8; Job 30.29 RV).
DRAGONS (plur.) would be *tanninim*.

owls
Better ' ostriches ' (RV). Jackals and ostriches are mentioned
together in 34.13; Mic. 1.8; Job 30.29 (RV).
21. Render 'the people whom I formed for myself, that
they may recount my praise' (cf. RV); the second clause
indicates purpose, and the whole is closely joined to the preceding verse.

The Exodus from Egypt was the occasion of the birth of
Israel as a people. It was the initial creative event in the
O.T. revelation, and it has much the same significance for
the Jews as the Resurrection of Christ has for Christians. In
the N.T. the prior event to the Resurrection is the Crucifixion.
In the O.T. the Exodus was preceded by the slavery in Egypt.
In both Testaments the creative events take place at the birth
of the Jewish and Christian Churches respectively. For a very
suggestive blending of the Exodus and Resurrection motifs in
Christian devotion see John Mason Neale's hymn 'The foe
behind, the deep before'. DI expected the new Exodus to be
the eschatological culmination of ·the faith of his fathers. In
one sense he was mistaken, but in another he was gloriously
right: what he depicted in mythological language as the end,
was, in its ultimate sequel and fulfilment, an even more
wonderful beginning.

SALVATION IS OF GOD'S GRACE, NOT THE REWARD OF SACRIFICIAL OFFERINGS
43.22-28

This passage is capable of two interpretations. Some think
that when Yahweh says that his people have not brought him
sacrificial offerings, he is only stating the fact that in the con-
ditions of the exile sacrificial worship was impossible. The
Jerusalem temple was in ruins and there was no altar in
Babylon. Others think that the reference is to the sacrifices
of pre-exilic times and that DI's attitude to sacrifice was just
as unfavourable as that of the great pre-exilic prophets (cf.
Amos 4.4f.; 5.21-25; Hos. 6.6; Isa. 1.10-15; Jer. 7.21-23; Mic.
6.6-8). There is much to be said for this second view. JACOB
. . . ISRAEL (v. 22) in DI generally stands for all Israel throughout its history, not merely for the generation of the exile, and
in vv. 26-28 the sinfulness of Israel is traced back to the very
beginnings of the nation. Moreover, the terms in which sacri-

fice is described seem depreciatory: SMALL CATTLE (v. 23);
FILLED ME (v. 24), literally 'drenched me' with fat; while the
reference to buying (*kanitha*) sweet cane (*kaneh*), with its
pungent alliteration (v. 24) is reminiscent of Jer. 6.20, where
Yahweh asks to what purpose is such costly fuss and labour.
The ME of v. 22 is emphatic: IT WAS NOT UPON *ME* THAT YOU
CALLED, O JACOB, TO THE POINT OF BECOMING WEARY OF ME,
O ISRAEL. YOU DID NOT BRING TO ME THE SMALL CATTLE OF
YOUR BURNT-OFFERINGS . . . I DID NOT IMPOSE UPON YOU THE
SLAVE-LABOUR OF BRINGING OFFERINGS, NOR WEARY YOU WITH
FRANKINCENSE . . . ON THE CONTRARY, IT WAS YOU WHO MADE
A SLAVE OF ME WITH YOUR SINS (a shattering anthropomor-
phism!), AND WEARIED ME WITH YOUR INIQUITIES! So far
from sacrifices being any passport to acceptance with God, I,
EVEN I, AM HE WHO WIPE OUT YOUR REBELLIONS FOR MY OWN
SAKE, because of what I am by my very nature, AND YOUR
SINS I WILL REMEMBER NO MORE. All is of divine initiative,
freely flowing from God's grace. This is Old as well as N.T.
doctrine. Then follows an invitation to judgement, so familiar
in DI (cf. 41.21-24; 43.9-13), but expressed here in almost
appealing terms (cf. 1.18). Indeed, the initiative is with Israel,
who may, so to speak, sue Yahweh if she will, and establish
her innocence (BE JUSTIFIED). Nay, the very father of the
nation (Jacob, cf. 58.14) was the first to sin, and those who were
the intermediaries between Yahweh and his people (kings,
priests, prophets, all) rebelled against him. Therefore he
defiled their kings, and gave Jacob to the ban, and made Israel
a taunt and a by-word.

25. blotteth
Lit. 'wipeth', cf. 25.8 (tears); II Kings 21.13 (a dish).

transgressions . . . sins
'Transgression' is hardly a strong enough word for the
Hebrew, which means 'rebellions' (similarly 'transgressed' in
v. 27 means 'rebelled'). Rebellion is a more flagrant offence
than trespass. The metaphor in the Hebrew 'sin' (verb and

noun) is that of missing the mark, deviation from the right
way. These two figures, rebellion and deviation, are the most
important for an understanding of sin in the O.T. Another
word is 'iniquity' (v.24), which also suggests 'deviation'.

27. teachers
Lit. 'interpreters' (RV, cf. Gen. 42.23), used here of the several
classes of intermediaries between Yahweh and Israel.

28. princes of the sanctuary
Lit. 'holy princes'. The words are used of the priests in the
late passage I Chron. 24.5 (RV), but here they refer to the
kings, who were sacramentally anointed for their high office.

given . . . to the curse
Put to the ban. Usually rendered in AV 'accursed thing', in
RV 'devoted thing'. For the operation of the ban in early
Israelite warfare see Josh. 6.17f.; 7; I Sam. 15 ('utterly
destroy', v. 3). Israel had not been utterly destroyed, and the
word is used here with some mitigation of its original terror.

V

ISAIAH 44

THE OUTPOURING OF THE SPIRIT FOR THE INCREASE OF ISRAEL
44.1-5

Like 43.1, which also follows a reproach, this begins with
BUT NOW, and is a message of consolation. Jacob-Israel is
Yahweh's servant, his chosen (41.8; 43.10). Yahweh made
him and formed him: the phrase FROM THE WOMB (also v. 24;
49.5) is reminiscent of Jer. 1.5, and means that Yahweh has
watched over his people ever since they began to be. MY
SERVANT and CHOSEN are repeated for emphasis in v.2. Once
more, Jacob is bidden not to fear and is further addressed by
the honourable name of Jeshurun. This is a poetical name
for Israel (Deut. 32.15; 33.5,26). It is derived from a root
meaning 'to be upright' and may be intended here as a contrast to Jacob ('deceiver', 'over-reacher', cf. Gen. 32.28).
There had been some danger that the Jewish community would
die out in exile: some were no doubt attracted by the
splendours of Babylon, and Jer. 29.6 is evidence that some
were unwilling to marry, hoping for a speedy return. The
pouring out of waters and streams (v. 3) has no reference here
to the transformation of the desert in preparation for the
return (as in 41.17f.; 43.19), but to an increase of the Jewish
population, which will be effected by the outpouring of
Yahweh's spirit. The operations of the SPIRIT of Yahweh were
from the earliest times characterized by invincible, dynamic
energy (cf. Judg. 6.34; 11.29). For the spirit as the creative
source of life see 42.5; Ps. 104.30; Ezek. 37.5 (RV marg.).

The figure here is of lush vegetation, like the poplars which lined the Babylonian canals (cf. Ps. 137.2). The only problem presented by the passage is whether v. 5 refers to the reclamation of defaulting Jews, or to proselytes from the heathen. If it is to the latter, the thought is introduced abruptly, and yet the language seems to require this interpretation. It may be translated: 'One shall say, "I belong to Yahweh", and another shall call himself by the name Jacob; yet another shall write on his hand, "To Yahweh", and give himself the surname "Israel".' (The italicized 'himself'— twice in the verse—can be integrated into the text by a simple and obvious change of vowel points.) This is much more naturally said of non-Israelites than of Israelites born. The reference in 'writing on the hand' is to the custom whereby a slave was tattooed or otherwise marked as the property of his master (Ex. 13.9,16; Ezek. 9.4; Rev. 7.3; 13.16).

It should be noted that nothing is said of any mass-conversion of the heathen: the proselyte adherents are to come in by ones and twos, as indeed they subsequently did. The passage is remarkable as being perhaps the earliest in which the Church is conceived of as a community which transcends the boundaries of race. Speaking generally, in the ancient world there was no thought of a supra-national or supra-racial faith. A man's religion was determined by his birth. Only in the N.T. does the Church become truly international. This was necessitated by the very nature of the Gospel, and it was prepared for by the Roman Empire, which admitted to its citizenship men of diverse races. It was anticipated and foreshadowed by the sixth-century Prophet.

YAHWEH ALONE IS GOD
44.6-8

This oracle again introduces Yahweh as KING (41.21; 43.15) of Israel, his REDEEMER (41.14). The expression YAHWEH OF HOSTS is frequent in the O.T., but in DI it is found only here

and in 45.13. In early times the HOSTS were the armies of
Israel; later they came to be thought of as the stars, the host
of heaven (see on 40.26), or as the angels. Apart from Yahweh
there is no God (cf. 43.10f.; 45.5f.,21). I AM THE FIRST, AND
I AM THE LAST is reminiscent of 41.4 (cf. 48.12). In the N.T.
it becomes 'I am the Alpha and the Omega' (the first and
last letters of the Greek alphabet; Rev. 1.8,17; 22.13). In v. 7
the gods (presumably) are again challenged to a legal process
(cf. 41.1-5,21-29; 43.9-13). The text of the verse has suffered
in transmission. From its first line the words 'let him stand
up' have fallen out, and may be restored from the LXX. In
the second half the words SINCE I APPOINTED THE ANCIENT
PEOPLE are an attempt to make' sense of very obscure Hebrew;
a simple but convincing emendation gives, 'Who announced
long ago things to come?' The last word in the verse (THEM)
should almost certainly be 'us'. The whole then reads: AND
WHO IS LIKE ME? LET HIM STAND UP, AND CALL OUT, AND
DECLARE, AND SET IT IN ORDER FOR ME. WHO ANNOUNCED LONG
AGO THINGS TO COME? AND THAT WHICH IS TO HAPPEN, LET
THEM TELL US. Here is a summary of legal procedure: counsel
rises in his place, raises his voice, declares and sets in order
(i.e. argues, cf. Job. 13.18; 33.5) his case. There can be no
answer to the challenge. Once more (v. 8) Israel is bidden not
to be in dread or fear. Then the verse proceeds (with some
change in the AV punctuation): DID I NOT DECLARE TO YOU
LONG AGO AND TELL YOU? AND YOU ARE MY WITNESSES (cf.
43.10ff.) WHETHER THERE IS ANY GOD BESIDE ME; INDEED,
THERE IS NO ROCK, I KNOW NONE. For 'Rock' as a divine
name cf. 26.4 RV; Deut. 32.30f.

THE STUPIDITY OF IDOLATRY
44.9-20

This passage is thought by many not to be from DI. The
reasons alleged are that it breaks the connexion between vv. 8
and 21, that it is in prose, that its detailed satire is not what

we should expect from the Prophet, is, indeed, rather beneath
his dignity, and that it contains grammatical peculiarities
which point to a different author. These reasons, though
cogent, are not decisive. It is not obvious that v. 21 is a
continuation of v. 8; there are traces of poetical rhythm in
the passage, and the subject does not call for sustained poetry.
Nor can we assume that the Prophet never descended from the
heights on which we generally encounter him. Idolatry had
its attractions and he may have felt it necessary to guard his
people against its allurements. He may even have borne
public witness to the Babylonians. While, therefore, we cannot assert with confidence that the passage *is* from DI, neither
can we say with certainty that it is *not* from him.

Whatever may be the origin of the passage, it is an expansion of 40.19f.; 41.6f.; 46.5ff. The stupidity of idolatry was
a favourite theme with Jewish apologists and propagandists;
cf. Jer. 10.1-16 (usually thought to be later than Jeremiah),
and especially Wisd. 13f., a magnificent passage which may be
described as an anti-philosophy of idolatry. Not that the
maker of an idol was ever quite so simple as to suppose that
that which *he* had made actually made *him*. But idolatry
has always gone hand in hand with superstition, and the
Prophet insists that superstition is essentially uncultured
and uncivilized: he who believes in a god that is apprehen-
sible to the physical senses is lacking in intelligence and
knowledge.

The argument of the passage is on the whole straight-
forward. The meticulous fuss of the whole procedure! The
material out of which the idol is made! Wood, the remnants
of which a man uses to light his fire and cook his food (this
last detail thrice repeated, vv. 15f.,19)! The climax of irony
comes when the accuser puts the indictment in the mouth of
the idol-worshipper, as if he would perforce acknowledge the
truth of it, if only he had any sense (v. 19)!

9. vanity
The same word as 'confusion' in 41.29 (see note there).

10. Translate: 'Whoever forms a god, or casts an image, is making a worthless thing'.

12. tongs
Better 'axe'. COALS always 'charcoal' in O.T.

13. rule . . , line
'line . . . pencil' (RV).

fitteth it with planes
Shapes it with a chisel (some kind of scraping tool).

14. strengtheneth
Better 'selects' or 'chooses'.
ASH better, some kind of fir (RV) or cedar.
16. Transpose the verbs EATETH and ROASTETH (with LXX). This gives a more logical order (cf. v. 19).

18. he hath shut their eyes, that they cannot see; and their hearts, that they cannot understand
Better, 'their eyes are smeared, that they cannot see. . . .' There is no suggestion that it is God who has smeared their eyes. The 'heart' in the O.T. is the seat of the intellect and will, the central organ of man's being (cf. v. 20). It occupied much the same place in Hebrew psychology as the brain does for us.

20. his soul
'himself'. There is no emphasis here upon soul as distinct from body.

RETURN UNTO ME!
44.21-23

These verses are one paragraph in the RV. Some scholars regard them as two short independent units, or perhaps fragments, vv. 21f. and 23. Some think that v. 21 is the original

continuation of v. 8; others that v. 23 is an introduction to
the divine declaration in vv. 24-28, on the ground that in O.T.
liturgies an oracle is sometimes prefaced by a hymn of praise
(as in Ps. 81, 95). Since the relation of the parts to their
contexts, and to one another, is uncertain, they are here for
convenience treated together.

In v. 21 it is not clear what is meant by THESE (RV 'these
things'). The pronoun may refer back to vv. 6-8, or to vv.
9-20, or it may be that the passage is a fragment which has
become detached from its original context. For THOU SHALT
NOT BE FORGOTTEN OF ME, which is grammatically difficult,
some of the versions read 'thou must not forget me' (cf. RV
marg.). The Hebrew consonants would give this translation
if differently vocalized, and we should then have a counterpart
to REMEMBER with which the verse begins. For I HAVE BLOTTED
(wiped) OUT, cf. 43.25. As quickly as clouds disperse before
the rising sun (Hos. 6.4; 13.3; Job 7.9; 30.15), so will Yahweh
wipe out Israel's rebellions and sins (cf. on 43.25)—the perfect
tense 'I have wiped out', is the so-called 'perfect of certainty'.
So far in the prophecy Yahweh's redemption of Israel has
referred to the coming release from Babylon. In this context
the word has perhaps a deeper meaning, that of redemption
from sin and guilt. In v. 23 the whole universe is summoned
to 'utter a ringing cry of praise' (SING) to Yahweh who has
DONE. The verb is used absolutely, without any accusative
of object. Similar examples are 41.4 ('done') and Ezek. 37.14
('performed'), where the word 'it' has no counterpart in the
Hebrew. The meaning is 'acted (decisively)'.

23. shout, ye lower parts of the earth
The verb translated SHOUT is commonly used of raising a blast
on the trumpet or horn. THE LOWER PARTS OF THE EARTH are
the underworld. In Ps. 6.5 'the grave' (RV 'Sheol'), the
underworld, is assumed to be outside the jurisdiction of
Yahweh, a place where no one gives him thanks. Here the
thought is in line with the late Ps. 139.8, where heaven and
earth and hell (Sheol) are all within his domain.

and glorified himself in Israel
The preposition IN means here ' by means of '; ' by means of
Israel he will get himself glory '.

YAHWEH IS THE ALMIGHTY CREATOR,
CYRUS IS HIS INSTRUMENT
44.24-28

Yahweh, Israel's Redeemer (see on 41.14), who formed him
from the womb (see on v. 2), is he who made all, who alone
stretched out the heavens (cf. 40.22) and spread (lit. ' beat ')
out the earth.   The verb ' beat out ' (as of metal) is related to
the noun ' firmament ' in Gen. 1.6 (see on 40.22).   For BY
MYSELF read ' Who was with me (when I did this)? ' (cf. RV).
The answer implied is ' No one! '   The participles should be
rendered by past tenses, ' made . . . stretched . . . spread
out ', since the references are to the original acts of creation.
In v. 25 Yahweh goes on to say that he FRUSTRATES (now
present tenses), i.e. makes ineffectual, the signs of the ' empty
talkers ', ' praters ' (cf. 16.6; Job 11.3).   They are the Babylonian astrologers, with their vain prognostications, and to all
intents and purposes they are LIARS.   The word is parallel with
DIVINERS, who practised divination by means of arrows
(belomancy) and inspecting the entrails of slaughtered animals
(haruspicy)—see the vivid picture in Ezek. 21.21f.   Yahweh
shows them to be fools, rather than MAKES THEM MAD; cf. THAT
MAKETH THEIR KNOWLEDGE FOOLISH at the end of the verse.
On the other hand, Yahweh confirms (v. 26) the word of his
servants (the plural SERVANTS is supported by some versions
and seems required by MESSENGERS in the parallel clause) and
brings to fulfilment (EVV ' performeth ') the collective
counsel (i.e. prophecies) of his messengers.   At this point the
passage becomes predictive.   Jerusalem shall again be inhabited,
the cities of Judah rebuilt, and the foundations of the temple
laid.   Even if the Prophet spoke disparagingly of sacrifice
(see on 43.22-25) this is not to say that he would be uncon-

cerned about the temple (cf. notes on 52.11-12). The temple
of any god was thought of first of all as his localized dwelling-
place on earth. In O.T. times men could hardly conceive of
God as present in their midst except in a temple, and it is
really a continuation of this idea which finds expression in
Rev. 21.22: 'I saw no temple therein: for the Lord God the
Almighty, and the Lamb, are the temple thereof'.

Such is the divine 'purpose' (v. 28). For this sense of the
word PLEASURE, which in later Hebrew came to have the
meaning 'purpose' or business', cf. 58.13; Prov. 31.13 (RV
marg.); Eccl. 3.1,17; 8.6. Yahweh's agent is Cyrus, who has
already been referred to (41.1-4,25) and is now actually named.
Yahweh calls him MY SHEPHERD. 'Shepherd' (verb and noun)
when used metaphorically in the O.T. always signifies 'rule',
'ruler'; Israel is 'the people of his pasture, the sheep of his
hand' (Ps. 95.7), and the business of the king is to feed the
sheep; cf. II Sam. 5.2; 7.7; Ps. 78.72; Ezek. 34. The words, MY
SHEPHERD can be vocalized to mean 'my friend', but 'shepherd' gives an entirely suitable meaning here.

27. This verse reads oddly in the present connexion. It
has been related to the story, told by Herodotus, that the armies
of Cyrus captured Babylon by diverting the course of the
Euphrates and marching along its dry bed. The story is now
regarded as a legend, since the Persian army entered Babylon
unopposed. Moreover, the word DEEP means 'ocean-deep'.
It is almost certain that the word has a mythological reference,
which is explained in the comment on 51.9f.

VI

ISAIAH 45

CYRUS THE MESSIAH
45.1-8

In the preceding section Cyrus has been designated Yahweh's 'shepherd', a regal title; here he is called his Messiah (ANOINTED ONE). Messiah was a title of the Hebrew kings: I Sam. 24.6 (Saul); II Sam. 19.21 (David); Ps. 2.2; 18.50 (David's dynasty). In later times it was used of the high priest (Lev. 4.3), who succeeded to some of the functions of the pre-exilic kings, and once of the patriarchs (Ps. 105.15), who were thought of as anointed kings. Somewhat strangely, the word is never used in the O.T. of the future Messianic king (Dan. 9.25f. refers to the high priest, cf. RV), though there is no reason to doubt that the Messianic king of 9.6f.; 11.1-9 and similar passages was to be an anointed king. The use of the title of Cyrus, a non-Israelite king, is unique, the nearest approach to it being Jer. 25.9; 27.6; 43.10, where Nebuchad-rezzar is called 'my servant'. We can only suppose that prior to the exile Messianic dogma had not yet become rigid, or that the Prophet was introducing an entirely new feature into it. There is probably some truth in both these alternatives, though Deut. 17.15 lays it down that the Israelites must not appoint a non-Israelite as their king. The rule of Cyrus, of course, was not of their appointing, and they had no choice but to accept it. That, however, was not DI's position: he appears at this stage to have welcomed Cyrus, to have thought of him as Yahweh's vice-gerent on earth, and even (v. 3) expected him to be a convert to Judaism.

The phrase WHOSE RIGHT HAND I HAVE HOLDEN is used of
Israel in 41.13; 42.6, and indicates a very intimate relation
to Yahweh. In Babylonia kings were said to grasp the hands
of the god Marduk at their accession, and there is actually
extant an inscription of Cyrus in which he says that Marduk (!)
took him by the hand and called him by name (cf. v. 3 here) and
gave him rule over the entire world. Since this inscription is
later than the fall of Babylon, DI cannot have borrowed from
it. Nor is its language borrowed from DI. Evidently the
Prophet was using the court-language of Babylonia and Persia.

The triumph of Cyrus is to be effected by Yahweh, who
will LOOSE THE LOINS OF KINGS, meaning that he will render
them helpless (cf. Job 12.21—RV: to gird up one's loins was
to prepare for strenuous activity, I Kings 18.46; II Kings
4.29; I Pet. 1.13; so here, v. 5, Yahweh is to GIRD Cyrus).
Doors and gates will be opened before him and no hindrances
of nature will impede his progress. The doors and bars that
guard the secret underground treasures of Babylon will be
hewn down. All this THAT THOU MAYEST KNOW THAT I AM
YAHWEH, THAT CALL THEE BY THY NAME, THE GOD OF ISRAEL;
a thought of incredible daring, that it is the God of an insignificant captive people who will lavish victory upon the world-
conqueror! Not only so, it is all for the sake of this same
captive people; though yet again, not for their sake alone, but
that the whole world may know, from the farthest east to the
farthest west, THAT THERE IS NONE BESIDE ME: I AM YAHWEH
AND THERE IS NONE ELSE. The next verse (7), I FORM THE
LIGHT, AND CREATE DARKNESS: I MAKE PEACE, AND CREATE
EVIL, has been thought to contain a stricture upon the native
religion of Cyrus (assuming, what is not certain, that he was
a Zoroastrian). According to Zoroastrianism there were two
creators, the one, Ahura Mazda, being responsible for the
beneficent things in the world, the other, Ahriman, for the evil.
It would, however, have been extremely maladroit of the
Prophet to engage in polemic against the faith of Cyrus, nor
should the text be understood in that sense: EVIL is calamity,
as in Amos 3.6. The O.T. has no hesitation in ascribing all

happenings in nature to the personal agency of Yahweh, though this is not the place to enter into a discussion of what for modern minds is a difficulty.

Verse 8, if not an independent fragment, may be taken as a hymnic conclusion to the preceding. The text of the middle part of the verse (note the unrelated pronoun THEM) is in some disorder, and the fact that DSI is also defective points to some deep-seated corruption. RIGHTEOUSNESS is the object of both DROP DOWN and POUR DOWN. It is here synonymous with 'salvation', both words having the sense of 'deliverance', 'victory' (see on 41.2, and cf. II Kings 5.1, where the Hebrew word 'salvation' is rendered by AV 'deliverance' and by RV 'victory').

The predictions in these verses were not fulfilled in the way the Prophet expected. Babylon was not entered forcibly, nor was it destroyed. Cyrus, as his own inscription testifies, did not become a convert to Judaism. For the problem raised by this non-, or only partial, fulfilment of the prophecy, see Introduction, *The Fulfilment of the Prophecy*, pp. 22ff.

1. the two-leaved gates
There is no particular significance about this (RV has 'doors' simply). The reference is to swinging doors, which could be barred. The GATE of a city was a larger structure than a 'door', and may be pictured as a gateway comprising posts, masonry, and the open space (corresponding to the 'square' of a modern city) to which it gave access (cf. Neh. 7.3; 13.19).

WOE UNTO HIM WHO WOULD CRITICIZE YAHWEH'S DECISIONS!
45.9-13

The closing verse of this paragraph indicates that there must have been some among the exiles who criticized the Prophet for asserting that Cyrus was the Messiah. The passage is ironical. Nothing is more passive than clay in the hands of the potter.

The man who 'goes to law' (STRIVETH is here a forensic term)
with his Maker is a mere earthen vessel among countless other
potsherds! (cf. RV). Can anything be more stupid or irrele-
vant than that a man should demand to know of a father,
'What begettest thou?' or of a mother, 'With what travailest
thou?' The imperatives ASK and COMMAND in v. 11 are the
climax of irony: cf. Moffatt's translation, 'Would you dictate
to me about my work?' The text of v. 11 is probably in some
disorder: the word THINGS-TO-COME in the Hebrew precedes
'ask me', and should perhaps to taken with what precedes.
This conjecture is now confirmed by DSI, which reads, 'Thus
saith Yahweh, the Holy One of Israel (these words being
inserted above the line by a later hand), who formed the future
(THINGS TO COME): Ask me about my sons, and about the
work of my hands command me!' Yahweh made everything
in earth and heaven—the anthropomorphism EVEN MY HANDS
emphasizes the 'I' immediately preceding, and at the same
time continues the figure of the potter and the clay. He has
raised up Cyrus IN RIGHTEOUSNESS, i.e. intentionally and for
a definite and righteous purpose (cf. 42.6). The concluding
words, NOT FOR PRICE NOR REWARD, are difficult to reconcile
with 43.3f. We must either suppose that the Prophet was not
concerned to be consistent, or that, like Homer, he was quite
capable of 'nodding' occasionally. All attempts to resolve the
inconsistency are forced, and we must conclude that the funda-
mental truths of prophecy were not dependent upon exact
precision in matters of detail.

9. or thy work, He hath no hands?
Better, perhaps, 'or his (the potter's) work, Thou hast no
hands?' HANDS here means power or skill.

CAPTIVES FROM EGYPT AND ETHIOPIA
45.14-17

The first verse of this passage is obviously related to 43.3
(which see). Its precise meaning is uncertain, the question
being the destination of the captive Africans. There are two
possible answers. One is that it is to the Jews, or perhaps to
Zion-Jerusalem, that the captives shall deliver themselves and
their tribute. This is the interpretation required by the word
THEE as it is now vocalized in the Hebrew: it is feminine and
must refer either to the Jews or to Jerusalem (peoples and cities
are commonly feminine gender in Hebrew). It is supported
by ch. 18, which speaks of a people from 'beyond the rivers
of Ethiopia', a people 'tall and smooth' (so RV rightly, vv.
2,7; cf. MEN OF STATURE here), who are to bring tribute to
Yahweh at Mount Zion. A serious difficulty to this interpretation is that the Sabeans are to come IN CHAINS. This difficulty
is obviated if we accept a very old, and recently revived, interpretation of the passage, viz. that the spoils of Africa are to
be handed over to Cyrus. This is what we should expect from
43.3 and is entirely in harmony with the present chapter, in
which Cyrus figures so prominently. That THEE according to
the present vowel pointing is feminine is not a serious objection: Hebrew was originally written without vowels, and the
consonants in UNTO THEE can as well be 'pointed' masculine
as feminine, so making the word refer to Cyrus. A possible
objection is that the captives are said to 'prostrate themselves'
(EVV FALL DOWN) and 'pray' (EVV MAKE SUPPLICATION) to
their captor. But this objection is not decisive in view of
Dan. 2. 46f.; Acts 14.13f.; I Cor. 14.25, especially if it is
remembered that the captives were heathen, accustomed to
pray to all sorts of divinities, even human 'gods' such as the
Egyptian Pharaoh.

Verses 15-17 are best understood as an utterance of the
Prophet, who marvels at the wondrous ways of Yahweh.
VERILY THOU ART A GOD THAT HIDEST THYSELF, O GOD OF

ISRAEL, SAVIOUR! SAVIOUR here is used absolutely, almost as
a proper name, as in 43.11. Nowhere in the O.T. is the
thought of the 'hidden' God, the *deus absconditus* of theology,
so plainly stated as here. In some ways it is so un-Hebrew
that many scholars, upon very slight textual evidence, are
encouraged to alter the text to read 'in thee (i.e. Israel) God
hides himself', and put the words into the mouth of the
Sabeans. In reality, the thought of God as 'hidden', notwithstanding that he is revealer, is by no means unfamiliar in
the O.T.; cf. passages like Ps. 97.2 and the story of Yahweh's
placing Moses in the cleft of a rock and covering him with
his hand to shield him from the untempered rays of the divine
glory, Ex. 33.17-23. That God is *deus absconditus* is a necessary corollary of any doctrine of divine transcendence. There
is a sense in which nature, with all its mingled revelation and
mystery, is a necessary barrier between God and ourselves,
lest we should be blinded by excess of light; cf. Browning,
Bishop Blougram's Apology, the lines beginning 'Pure faith
indeed—you know not what you ask', and Cowper's 'God
moves in a mysterious way . . . Deep in unfathomable
mines . . .'

THE WHOLE WORLD SHALL
ACKNOWLEDGE ISRAEL'S GOD
45.18-25

In this passage the conclusion of the doctrine of one only
God is drawn, viz. that there is only one true religion. The
hymnic introduction (v. 18) is even more than usually elabo-
rate: Yahweh CREATED the heavens and FORMED the earth and
firmly established it. It is an orderly creation; not 'a waste'
(so read for IN VAIN, as in RV; the word is used in Gen. 1.2
of the chaos that preceded the creation, where AV has 'without form', and RV 'waste') but a habitable world. Not only
is Yahweh's creation orderly but his word is clear (v. 9). He
has never spoken in secret, IN A PLACE OF THE LAND OF DARK-

NESS (RV). Here also reference may be made to Gen. 1.2, where waste and darkness are together descriptive of the primeval chaos. (It should perhaps be noted that in the O.T. there is as yet no doctrine of creation out of nothing.) For IN VAIN we should probably read 'in the void' or 'waste'— the word is a noun, the same as in v. 18. That Yahweh has never spoken in secret is no contradiction of what is said of him in v. 15, that he 'hides himself'. Any doctrine of revelation assumes that God is unknown and unknowable except insofar as he chooses to reveal himself, that man cannot by searching find out God (Job 11.7). Even the most intimate human associates do not penetrate to the innermost recesses of each other's personality. What is meant by the text is that Yahweh does not make himself deliberately obscure, so that men are driven to 'seek' him by superstitious, or occult, or orgiastic means. He speaks righteousness and declares what is right. He is not, like the gods of the heathen, accessible only to those who know the techniques of divination or are expert in the elaborations of ritual. As a great German commentator (Volz) has put it: 'O.T. religion is at once grand and simple; it is the religion of the layman', the religion of Abraham, Moses, and the prophets, and, we may add, of the great rabbis.

From this point the divine self-predication widens out into a summons to the nations to ASSEMBLE YOURSELVES AND COME. It is a summons to something like the now familiar judicial convocation (cf. on 41.21-24; 43.9-13; 44.6-8), though the tone is less menacing. Those that are ESCAPED OF THE NATIONS are presumably those who shall have survived the world-shattering events which are the theme of the preceding chapters. The two themes of the folly of idolatry and the total inability of the gods to foretell the future are repeated, but there is a recognition that what the heathen have done, they have done in ignorance rather than out of wilful wickedness—THEY HAVE NO KNOWLEDGE THAT 'carry' (so translate with RV) THE WOOD OF THEIR GRAVEN IMAGE; the reference is to the custom of carrying the statues of the gods in procession on cultic occasions (cf. 46.1f.) Note the remarkable collocation, A JUST

(better 'righteous') GOD AND A SAVIOUR (v. 21). There is no
contradiction, let alone contrast, between these two great
attributes; indeed, it is precisely because God is righteous that
he is Saviour (see the magnificent development of this theme
by St. Paul in Rom. 3). Even justice, a less exalted concept
than righteousness, is tempered with mercy. In Scripture the
righteousness of God is to be defined in the light of his activity
as Saviour, and it becomes more and more pregnant with
meaning as his saving purpose for the world unfolds.

In v. 22 the summons becomes an appeal, though the verbs
are still in the imperative mood, as indeed they are in the
'Come unto me' of Jesus (Matt. 11.28), which, as in the
present passage, follows a divine self-predication. TURN UNTO
ME AND LET YOURSELVES BE SAVED, ALL THE ENDS OF THE
EARTH: FOR I AM GOD, AND THERE IS NONE ELSE. It is one of
the high peaks of O.T. religion. Notice the stress on the
individual: 'EVERY KNEE . . . EVERY TONGUE'. It is not
merely a mass conversion that is envisaged, but an experience
into which men will enter as individuals. In the New
Covenant passage in Jeremiah (31.31-34) the covenant is
announced as 'with the house of Israel and with the house of
Judah', though the terms in which it is expanded (vv. 33f.)
show that it was to be made effective by the regeneration of
individual Israelites. The present passage marks an advance
even upon that, since it embraces all individual Gentiles. In
vv. 24f. Yahweh is referred to in the third person and it may
be that the conclusion is a later addition (note the awkward
AGAINST HIM, presumably Israel). On the other hand, it is
usual for the Prophet's thought to begin and end with Israel,
Yahweh's witnesses to the heathen world.

24. Surely, shall ONE say, in the LORD have I righteousness and strength

Better, 'Only in the Lord, shall one say unto me, is righteousness and strength' (RV). The text is uncertain.

VII

ISAIAH 46

THE GOD WHO CARRIES AND GODS WHICH MUST BE CARRIED
46.1-13

This chapter is best treated as a unity, notwithstanding that v. 3 begins with a new address and vv. 5-7 (or 8?) are somewhat loosely related to their context. The theme is the contrast between Yahweh who carries his people as a father carries his children (FROM THE WOMB, v. 3) and the Babylonian gods which are lifeless blocks needing to be carried about by their distraught worshippers. It is a theme which is homiletically most suggestive, and the reader is recommended to study Sir George Adam Smith's classic exposition of it. 'The truth is this: it makes all the difference to a man how he conceives his religion—whether as something that he has to carry, or as something that will carry him' (*The Book of Isaiah*, vol. II, 2nd ed., p. 198).

Bel and Nebo (Nabu) were the two most prominent gods in the Babylonian pantheon. Bel, the equivalent of the Hebrew Baal, means 'lord', and was a title of Marduk. Nabu, which means 'speaker', was the son of Bel-Marduk and was worshipped at Borsippa. It is probable that Nabu was the patron-god of the Chaldean kings, since the three most important of them, Nabopolassar, Nebuchadrezzar, and Nabonidus, had names compounded with his. The Prophet pictures the gods being loaded on the backs of pack-animals, presumably to be carried into safety before the approaching conqueror. The tenses throughout are present, but the scene is depicted as in the near future. That the passage is predictive, not a description after the event, is clear from the fact that there was no stampede to evacuate the city of its gods before it fell to Cyrus. Nor did Cyrus banish the gods from their temples; instead, he ascribed his conquest to Marduk, and besought all the gods to ask Bel and Nabu daily to grant him long life. The translation CARRIAGES (v.1) is incorrect: the word means 'things carried' (cf. RV). Even so, the second person plural pronoun YOUR is unrelated; the versions read 'their' and the text is probably corrupt. Nor is it clear whether THEY who cannot deliver the burden into safety are the gods themselves or those (their worshippers, or the pack-animals?) that carry them. But the general picture of panic and exhaustion is sufficiently clear.

In the magnificent contrast which follows (vv. 3f.) there is some emphasis upon Yahweh's carrying of individual Israelites, EVEN TO HOAR HAIRS; cf. Ps. 71.18. Moreover, Yahweh bears his people from the cradle to the grave. There is no specific reference in THE REMNANT OF THE HOUSE OF ISRAEL to the exiles of the old Northern Kingdom. O HOUSE OF JACOB, AND ALL THE REMNANT OF THE HOUSE OF ISRAEL means Israel as a whole, including its individual units.

Verses 5-7 are in form similar to 40.18-20, a rhetorical question, TO WHOM WILL YE LIKEN ME? followed by description of the stupidity of idolatry. The sense in v. 6 is something like, 'To think that people can be so foolish as to pay out money for the making of an idol, and then call the manufactured article a god!'

Verses 8-13 appear to be addressed to rebellious Israelites (TRANSGRESSORS, cf. on 43.25). The theme is similar to that in 45.9-13, which inveighs against those who criticize Yahweh for accomplishing his purpose through Cyrus. The translation SHEW YOURSELVES MEN is very uncertain. Various emendations have been suggested, such as 'show discernment', or 'be ashamed', but the text can bear the sense of 'place yourselves on a firm foundation'. There follows an appeal to the fulfilment of previous prophecies, similar to 41.26; 42.9; 43.9; 44.7;

45.21. What Yahweh has purposed (for PLEASURE in the sense of 'purpose' see on 44.28) shall come to pass. The RAVENOUS BIRD from the east is once more Cyrus. The Hebrew word (*ayit*) is short, sharp, and imitative of the scream of a bird of prey. The figure is similar to that in Ezek. 17.3, where Nebuchadrezzar is called a great vulture. The last two verses (12f.) present a difficulty, because Yahweh appears to offer RIGHTEOUSNESS to a people who are STOUTHEARTED (=obstinate) and far from it, and who presumably would not welcome it. Accordingly, some would alter STOUTHEARTED to 'fainthearted', on the basis of the LXX. There is no need for this if we take RIGHTEOUSNESS and SALVATION as almost synonyms in the sense of 'victory', 'deliverance' (see on 45.8).

VIII

ISAIAH 47

BABYLON'S PRIDE AND HUMILIATION
47.1-15

This chapter is a unity, with fairly clearly defined sub-sections or strophes. In the first section (vv. 1-4) Babylon is described as a luxury-loving lady who shall be degraded to the status of the meanest slave. In the second (vv. 5-7) she is a cruel tyrant; in the third (vv. 8-10) a sorceress whose misdeeds shall be requited. In the remainder of the chapter the divisions are less clear: in vv. 11-12 no wiles or enchantments shall be able to ward off her doom; in vv. 13-15 she is left forsaken by all in whom she trusted. The tone is dignified, ironical rather than revengeful. Babylon's ill-treatment of the Jews is indeed described, but it does not stand in the foreground. The indictment is directed rather against her overweening pride and utter heartlessness. There is a general similarity to chapters 13-14. These chapters became models for descriptions of the world-tyrant, 'Antichrist', like the 'little horn' in the book of Daniel, and 'Babylon' (=Rome) in the book of Revelation (cf. especially Rev. 17.5). Tyrants are much the same everywhere and in every age. That is why enthusiasts are able to discover predictions of Hitler and his like in the pages of Scripture.

1-4. Babylon is personified as a young woman (cf. 1.8; 37.22, Zion; 23.12, Sidon; Jer. 46.11, Egypt), similarly to our 'Britannia', 'Marianne'. She is bidden to descend and sit 'throneless' for AV *THERE IS* NO THRONE) in the dust (a sign of mourning, cf. 3.26). She shall exchange her pampered

harem-life for that of a slave. To grind with the millstones
was the task of the lowest menial (cf. Ex. 11.5), unencumbered
by headtires and flowing skirts—so RV 'remove thy veil, strip
off the train' (cf. Jer. 13.18 RV), for AV UNCOVER THY LOCKS,
MAKE BARE THE LEG. Instead of being carried about by
palanquin or boat, the delicately nurtured lady must ford
rivers as best she can. The second half of v. 3 is almost certainly corrupted: for I WILL NOT MEET *THEE AS* A MAN. *AS
FOR* OUR REDEEMER, we should read with LXX, 'I will not be
entreated, saith our redeemer . . .'

5-7. The repeated SIT is followed by IN SILENCE, AND ENTER
INTO DARKNESS, like one terrified by the threat of divine
judgement (cf. I Kings 21.27) or anxious to hide himself from
God (cf. Ps. 139.11). No more shall Babylon be called THE
MISTRESS OF KINGDOMS. Verse 6 is strongly reminiscent of
Jer. 12.7. Like Assyria (10.5-15), Babylon has exceeded her
commission as Yahweh's instrument for the chastisement of
his people. This is summed up in the accusation UPON THE
AGED (SO RV) HAST THOU VERY HEAVILY LAID THY YOKE, the
refinement of cruelty. In v. 7 the words SO THAT are best
omitted: THESE THINGS refers to the immediately preceding
description of Babylon's conduct. We get a double impression
of Babylon's behaviour towards the Jews. There is no reason
to suppose that the contemporary descriptions in Lam. 4-5 are
exaggerated, while other passages in DI speak of ill-usage
(49.26; 51.13,17-23). On the other hand it would seem that the
exiles were allowed the right of free assembly (Ezek. 8.1; 14.1)
and that they had a measure of personal freedom (Jer. 29.5f.).
There is probably truth in both these descriptions; tyrants have
never been squeamish in their attitude to conquered peoples.

8-10. The words THEREFORE NOW draw the consequences
from what precedes. The crowning indictment is that Babylon,
like Nineveh (Zeph. 2.15) has presumed to set herself up in the
place of God.

I am, and there is none else beside me
repeated in v.10, is language only proper to God, cf. 45.5f. By

widowhood and loss of children (cf. Rev. 18.7f.) is meant
military catastrophe, which shall overtake Babylon 'completely' (AV IN THEIR PERFECTION, RV 'in their full measure '),
this 'in spite of' (RV 'despite of' is better than AV FOR) the
multitude of her sorceries. Not even Babylon 'trusted in
wickedness'; the meaning is that she 'felt herself secure' in
her wickedness. Her very wisdom and knowledge gave her
a false confidence.

11-12. The tyrant's fate is described in a crescendo of
alliterative words—*rāʿāh*, 'evil', 'calamity', *hōwāh*, 'mischief', 'ruin', *shōʿāh*, 'desolation', 'devastation'. The end
shall be sudden. For FROM WHENCE IT RISETH translate 'how
to charm it away' (RV marg.), or, perhaps, with a slight textual
change, 'how to bribe it off', which would be an excellent
parallel to PUT IT OFF, literally 'propitiate' or 'buy off'. The
last word in v. 12 means properly 'to strike terror' (RV
marg.): the evils of the preceding verse are pictured as demons
such as Babylonian sorcerers might hope to scare away with
incantations and din.

13-15. The very multitude of Babylon's 'counsellors' (so
read perhaps for COUNSELS) only leaves her in the greater confusion. Such are the ASTROLOGERS (lit. those who divide the
heavens [into constellations]), those who gaze at the stars, and
those who from the monthly calendars decide from what
quarters luck and ill-fortune come. Let them stand up and
save her! In vain: they themselves shall be as stubble
devoured by fire. It shall not be a comfortable fire at which
to warm themselves or to sit by (grim scorn!), but a raging
furnace. It shall be a case of save himself who can! Babylon
shall be left alone to her fate. The word MERCHANTS in the
last verse introduces a new feature into the chapter. It is
awkwardly placed and would read better after UNTO THEE.
Perhaps it is a gloss. A very slight textual change would give
the meaning 'thy charmers', though Nah. 3.16 (referring to
Nineveh) is evidence of the crowds of merchants who thronged
the bazaars of great cities.

IX

ISAIAH 48

THE PURPOSE OF PREDICTION, TO FORESTALL APOSTASY
48.1-11

The main argument of this section is that Yahweh long ago predicted the disaster which would overtake his people, in order that when it came they should have no excuse for attributing it to any other agency, human or divine. Similarly now, on the eve of their liberation, he predicts NEW THINGS, this for the sake of his NAME and because he knows how prone his people are to misinterpret the courses of events.

The passage has occasioned a good deal of perplexity to commentators. It is even harsher in tone than 43.22-28 and 46.8, and seems hardly consistent with the message of 'the prophet of consolation'. Nor are the strictures in it addressed to a section only of the exiles, like those in 45.9-11, but apparently to the whole nation, which is even accused of idolatry. Indeed, the general tone, and even some details, are strongly reminiscent of Ezekiel. Accordingly, some have denied the passage to DI. Others have supposed that the original oracle has been interpolated, so that in its present form it consists of a genuine Deutero-Isaianic nucleus together with a kind of interlinear commentary. This type of interpretation has become quite common and a good example of it is to be seen in Moffatt's translation, which brackets vv. 1b,2,4,5b,7b,8b-10, and the words HOW SHOULD *MY NAME* BE POLLUTED? in v. 11, as secondary. Even if this interpretation should be the right one, it may be pointed out that the passage is extant in

Holy Scripture as we have it, and that, however interesting
questions of literary analysis may be in themselves, it is with
the present form of the text that we have to do. The most
recent commentators, however, are decidedly inclined to the
view that the passage, much as we have it, is from DI. It is
pointed out that he was no mild enthusiast, that he certainly
encountered opposition (see on 45.9-11), and that he was
deeply concerned to penetrate to the underlying causes of
things. Moreover, it is difficult to see what motive a later
scribe could have in turning his mildness into harshness,
especially when the general tendency seems to have been to
tone down the asperities of the prophets. The suggestion has
been made that the passage is an address actually given by the
Prophet on one of the days of penitence and fasting which it is
known that the exiles observed in Babylon (cf. Zech. 7.3-5).
Whether this is so or not, the suggestion is a valuable one. It
would be surprising if the Prophet of the exile did not exercise
a real public ministry, as his predecessors had done. We know
so little about him that we can easily think of him as a poet
and writer who did all his work in academic seclusion. This
passage may afford some insight into his relations with his
contemporaries and the difficulties he encountered.

The address (v. 1) is to THE HOUSE OF JACOB, WHICH ARE
CALLED BY THE NAME OF ISRAEL, AND CAME OUT FROM THE
WATERS OF JUDAH. JUDAH is otherwise only mentioned twice
in DI (40.9; 44.26—both times 'the cities of Judah'). The
WATERS of Judah may perhaps be explained from Deut. 33.28;
Ps. 68.26 (RV), where the ancestor Jacob-Israel is compared
to a fountain. A slight textual change would give 'bowels'
(cf. Gen. 15.4). Some of the rabbis took WATERS as a
euphemism in this sense. To 'swear' (Deut. 6.13; 10.20) and
'make mention' (Ps. 20.7 RV) were cultic acts, and support
the suggestion that this oracle was delivered at some assembly
for worship. THE HOLY CITY (v. 2) came to be a common
designation of Jerusalem (Neh. 11.1; Dan. 9.24; Matt. 4.5;
27.53), the name (*el-quds*) by which it is still called by Muslims.
It was supposed in the ancient world that the fortunes of

nations depended upon the power of their gods and that their fate reflected the struggles of the gods in the supernatural world (cf. Dan. 10.13,20f.). Hence, if a people suffered disaster, it was because its god had been defeated by his divine antagonists. Therefore, if Yahweh had not announced the exile beforehand, and that it was he who was bringing it about, his people would have assumed that Bel-Marduk was stronger than he (vv. 3ff.). Verse 4 is reminiscent of earlier prophetic denunciations (Ex. 32.9; Deut. 9.6,13; Jer. 3.3; Ezek. 3.7ff.). Verse 5 accuses the nation of idolatry. There is no evidence that idolatry was at all widespread among the exiles, and since the denunciation is of the whole nation, it must be supposed that the Prophet is speaking of idolatry in pre-exilic times (cf. Jer. 44.15-17). This would explain the severity of his language: he is passing judgement upon the whole record of his people (cf. v.8). The word DECLARE (v. 6) is best understood in the sense of 'recognize', 'admit'.

Verse 6b announces NEW THINGS FROM THIS TIME (i.e. from now on). These NEW THINGS are contrasted with the FORMER THINGS (v. 3), the predictions of the pre-exilic prophets, which were made ' long ago ' (this is the meaning of the word rendered FROM THE BEGINNING by AV in vv. 3 and 7). *They* are created NOW, and not long ago, and the people had never heard of them before. This statement is practically conclusive for an exilic date for DI (see Introduction, pp. 15f).

The emphasis in FOR MY NAME'S SAKE (v. 9) is rather different from that in the similar phrase in 43.25. There it is on the divine grace; here it is upon the divine honour. The thought is very similar to that in Ezek. 36.22, viz. that if Yahweh had suffered his people to be obliterated, his NAME would have become a by-word among the heathen. Instead, therefore, of ' cutting off' Israel, he has REFINED her. The parallel word to REFINED is CHOSEN, which does not seem very appropriate. The change of a single letter would give ' tested ' (cf. RV marg. ' tried '). It has long been suspected that this was the original reading, and it now receives manuscript support from DSI. For ' refine ' and ' test ' in parallelism see

Jer. 9.7; Zech. 13.9, and for THE FURNACE OF AFFLICTION cf.
the 'iron furnace' of the Egyptian bondage (Deut. 4.20; I Kings
8.51; Jer. 11.4). If the release from Babylon is a second
Exodus, the exile was a second Egyptian bondage. Therefore
Yahweh will 'act' (for this absolute sense of DO see on 44.23).

10. with silver

is meaningless. RV has 'as silver'. The proper meaning of
the preposition is 'for'. Yahweh has not refined his people
for any advantage or profit that might accrue to himself from
the process!

11. How should MY NAME be polluted?

Lit. 'How is it profaned?' The passive verb has no subject.
The words are prose in between two lines of poetry. DSI has
'how should I be profaned?' The words were originally, perhaps, a marginal comment, but one entirely appropriate to the
context.

YAHWEH, THE LORD OF ALL, HAS CALLED CYRUS
48.12-16

This is a short 'disputation' asserting that it is Yahweh alone
who has raised up Cyrus (cf. 45.12f.). It is addressed to Jacob-
Israel, MY CALLED ONE (cf. 43.1), a title with much the same
meaning as 'my chosen'. Yahweh is THE FIRST AND ALSO
THE LAST (41.4; 44.6), the creator who laid the foundation of
the earth and SPREAD OUT (RV) the heavens, once for all. He
is also Lord of history: WHEN I CALL UNTO THEM, THEY STAND
UP TOGETHER (present tenses, cf. 40.26). Israelites are still
addressed in v. 14. Some MSS. read 'you' for THEM, but
there has never been any question of Israelites predicting the
future; THEM, although an unrelated pronoun, must refer to
the 'no-gods'. Verse 14b, as it stands, should be translated, HE
WHOM YAHWEH LOVES SHALL ACCOMPLISH HIS PURPOSE (cf. RV

marg.). The name Yahweh is omitted in LXX, which is more
natural since it is Yahweh who is speaking. Perhaps the
original text was 'He whom I love shall accomplish my purpose'. The word 'he-whom-I-love' is the same as is used
of Abraham ('my friend') in 41.8. It indicates that Yahweh's
relation to Cyrus is intimate (cf. 44.28; 45.1), not simply an
external relation to a conqueror whom he uses as his agent.
The last clause of the verse is difficult: lit. AND HIS ARM ON
THE CHALDEANS. Perhaps we should read 'and (against) the
seed of the Chaldeans' (the words for 'seed' and 'arm' look
very much alike in Hebrew). Notice the four verbs in v. 15,
giving the impression of rapid, decisive action. The last clause
of v. 16 must be an utterance of the Prophet. It is awkwardly
constructed, in prose, and it is not clear whether AND HIS
SPIRIT is a second subject, or a second object, of SENT. RV
gives the literal rendering, AND NOW THE LORD YAHWEH HATH
SENT ME, AND HIS SPIRIT. It is the only certain reference of
the Prophet to himself, apart from 'and I said' (LXX) of 40.6,
and may well be a later insertion. It would be tempting to
take the whole of v. 16 as referring to the Prophet, were it not
much more natural to take the words I HAVE NEVER SPOKEN IN
SECRET as an utterance of Yahweh (cf. 45.19).

'HOW OFTEN WOULD I . . . !'
48.17-19

It is difficult to decide whether this passage looks to the past
or to the future, or, in other words, whether it is a reproach
or a (conditional) promise. Both AV and RV translate v. 18
by past tenses. RV marg. has, OH THAT THOU WOULDEST
HEARKEN . . . THEN SHOULD THY PEACE BE . . . That this is
a perfectly possible rendering is clear from the exactly similar
construction in 64.1, though if we continue the future reference
in the second clause and into v. 19, we should perhaps need
to alter the vowel points of the repeated HAD BEEN, to make it
mean 'would be'. On the whole, the past reference seems

preferable. Verse 19 is evidently reminiscent of the promises of numerous descendants to Abraham (Gen. 13.16; 22.17). The exiles, and the Prophet himself, must have been much exercised, as they pondered over the nation's past history and present doleful circumstances, to know why the promises had not been more adequately fulfilled. This passage supplies the answer: the nation had not profited by the teaching which would have led it in the way it should go. Not that prosperity (RIGHTEOUSNESS, v. 18; see on 41.2; 45.8) is exactly the reward of obedience. Religion is not morality. All is of God's grace. But without morality religion perishes. Yet even when we have read the passage as reproach rather than promise, the promise is still open, since mercy is ever renewed.

19. his name
LXX reads 'thy name'; but the reference can quite well be to SEED.

HOME FROM BABYLON!
48.20-22

Deliverance is so certain and so near that the Prophet cries 'Gó out from Bábylon, flée from the Chaldéans!' The sentences are appropriately short and sharp, with only two stresses each (the usual number is three). The summons to FLEE is to be interpreted in the light of Jer. 51.6 (cf. Rev. 18.4). The exiles, if they do not make haste, will be in a similar peril to Lot (Gen. 19.15ff); the destruction that is coming upon the city may overtake them. Even more important than that the exiles are free is the fact that it is Yahweh who has REDEEMED them, and they are to publish the glad tidings to all the world. And indeed, even if this second Exodus was less marvellous than the Prophet anticipated, it did excite wonder among the nations (Ps. 126.2). What follows (v. 21) is a recollection of the first Exodus (Ex. 17.6; Num. 20.11), which in itself is a sure promise for the second (cf. 41.18; 43.19f.). Verse 22 seems

out of place in this context. It is word for word the same as
57.21, except that it has 'Yahweh' for 'my God'. It is probable that it comes from the Trito-Isaianic circle, and that it
was intended to mark the close of the first half of DI's
prophecy. Another explanation is that v. 20 contains four
lines, v. 21 only three. A line may have been lost, and v. 22
added as compensation.

X

ISAIAH 49

THE SERVANT OF YAHWEH: HIS CALL TO BE A LIGHT TO THE HEATHEN
49.1-6

This is the second of the Servant Songs (see on 42.1-4). In it the speaker is the Servant himself and he addresses himself to the inhabitants of the farthest coastlands (see on 40.15), to whom he had already been commissioned (42.4). Yahweh has called him from the womb, a feature strongly reminiscent of Jer. 1.5. For an unspecified time he was kept in instant readiness for his task, like a sharp sword in the scabbard of the Divine Warrior, or a polished arrow concealed in his quiver (v. 2). The first part of the Song culminates in the statement, AND HE (Yahweh) SAID TO ME, THOU ART MY SERVANT, ISRAEL BY WHOM I WILL GET MYSELF GLORY. The AV takes ISRAEL as a vocative; it is better to take it as an extension of the predicate 'servant', as in RV, though the comma of the AV is to be preferred to the semicolon of RV. That the Servant should be called ISRAEL occasions considerable perplexity. It is true that outside the Songs Israel is called the Servant (see on 42.1-4), but everywhere else in the Songs the Servant is anonymous. This would not matter were it not that in v. 5 the Servant is represented as having a mission to Israel. How can Israel have a mission to Israel? Even if, as is grammatically possible though not very probable, it is Yahweh who is to bring Israel to himself in v. 5—translating BY BRINGING ISRAEL AGAIN TO HIMSELF—we are still left with the difficulty that in a passage in which the Servant is addressed as Israel,

Jacob-Israel is referred to by name in the third person. Many scholars accordingly delete ISRAEL in v. 3. But the textual evidence for this is limited to one MS. It is therefore better to keep to the text and translate THOU ISRAEL BY WHOM I WILL GET MYSELF GLORY. This would have some such sense as that the Servant is 'the true (embodiment of) Israel', and be consistent with an interpretation which would make the Servant either an individual, or a minority (remnant) within Israel. Many scholars would transpose v. 5b to follow v.3, translating 'and so I became honourable in the eyes of Yahweh and my God became my strength'. The words are bracketed in RV and are an awkward parenthesis in their present position.

In v. 4 the Servant speaks of fruitless labour which has exhausted his strength. In the light of vv. 5f. this labour would seem to have been amongst his own people. He is, however, confident that his 'just right' (see on 40.27) is safe with Yahweh and his 'recompense' (so RV; see on 40.10) with his God. But instead of discharging him from his calling, Yahweh, who never suffers his servants to discharge themselves (cf. Jer. 15.19; 20.7ff.), widens the scope of his mission to embrace all mankind. His mission so far had been TO BRING JACOB UNTO HIM, AND THAT ISRAEL SHOULD BE GATHERED TO HIM . . . TO RAISE UP THE TRIBES OF JACOB AND TO RESTORE THE PRESERVED (i.e. survivors) OF ISRAEL. This points to the Servant's task to Israel having been political as well as spiritual. Verse 6 appears to mean that the Servant is to leave uncompleted the work on which he had first been engaged, of restoring the political fortunes of Israel, and, like St. Paul (Acts 13.46; 18.6), turn to the Gentiles. The word 'also' should not be stressed; it is not even in the Hebrew, which only says 'so I make thee a light to the Gentiles, that my salvation may reach to the end of the earth' (cf. RV marg. for the translation of the last clause).

5. Though Israel be not gathered
Read with RV 'and that Israel be gathered unto him'. The Hebrew words 'not' and 'to him' sound exactly the same,

though they are spelt differently. If the negative is kept, the verb should be understood in the sense of 'gathered (up)' and so 'swept away'. This gives a good sense, but the RV reading is more natural.

THE WONDROUS REVERSAL OF ISRAEL'S FORTUNE
49.7-13

This passage is taken by some to be a continuation of the preceding Servant Song, by others as a separate Song. It has obvious similarities to 42.5-9 (which see), and it is probable that like that passage it originally referred to Israel, and was later referred to the Servant by the insertion of the words 'and I form (the word is the same as in 42.6, cf. RV marg. there) thee, and make thee a covenant-bond of the people', in v. 8. The opening words of v. 9 in the AV—THAT THOU MAYEST SAY TO THE PRISONERS, GO FORTH—read more into the Hebrew than is actually there. The literal translation is 'saying to them that are bound, Go forth', as in RV. The subject is Yahweh, and it is he also who is TO RAISE UP (i.e. resettle) THE LAND (of Palestine) AND MAKE (his people) INHERIT THE DESO-LATE HERITAGES (v. 8, cf. RV).

The introductory formula THUS SAITH YAHWEH occurs in both vv. 7 and 8, and v. 7 may be only a fragment. A wondrous reversal of fortune is in store for Israel. The phrase TO HIM WHOM MAN DESPISETH is literally 'to a despising of soul'. This is best explained from Ps. 17.9, where 'my deadly enemies' is literally 'my enemies against the soul'. Hence, here, 'to him who is deeply despised'. NATION is used in the general sense of 'people', as in 55.5; the word generally conveys some emphasis upon non-Hebrews. The reversal of Israel's fortune will excite amazement among Gentile kings and princes (cf. 52.15).

In vv. 9-11 the returning exiles are pictured as sheep with Yahweh as their shepherd and leader (cf. 40.10f.). There are

echoes, too, of the transformation of nature in 41.17-20; 43.19f.
The passage ends with a short hymn of praise similar to 42.8f.;
44.23; 45.8.

12. This verse would come more naturally after v. 18 and
may have stood there originally (cf. 60.4). SINIM is not China,
as was once thought, but the modern Assuan, in Upper Egypt,
near the first Nile Cataract. It is known that there was a considerable Jewish colony there, and in the early years of the
present century a number of papyrus documents (the Elephantine papyri) were discovered from which much has been learned
of their manner of life. The colony must have existed in DI's
time (cf. Jer. 44.1; Isa. 11.11, where Pathros = Upper Egypt).

THE REPOPULATION OF ZION
49.14-21

Verses 14-26 of this chapter contain three short poems on
related themes. Some scholars regard them as a single poem,
but it is perhaps better for purposes of exposition to treat
them as separate units. The introductory formula (FOR) THUS
SAITH (THE LORD) YAHWEH occurs at v. 22 and again at v. 25.

In vv. 14-21 the theme is Zion's lament that she is a wife
forsaken and forgotten by her husband (Yahweh; see on 40.2,
and cf. 50.1; 54.1-8) and bereaved of her children. She is
assured (v. 15) that Yahweh's love for her is more constant
and enduring than that of a mother for the child she has
borne and suckled (cf. Ps. 27.10), an unchanging love, 'Free
and faithful, strong as death' (Cowper). A still more anthropomorphic figure follows in v. 16, where Yahweh is a lover who
tattoos the name of his beloved upon the palms of his hands;
or perhaps, in the light of the parallel THY WALLS ARE CON-
TINUALLY BEFORE ME, the tattoo is a plan of the rebuilt city.
THY CHILDREN (v. 17) is an appropriate enough anticipation of
v. 18, but the word can be vocalized to mean 'builders'. This
would be an excellent antithetic parallel to DESTROYERS and it
is supported by 44.26,28; 45.13; 60.10. Verse 12, as already sug-

gested (see above), should perhaps come after 18a.   The figure
of Zion putting on her restored children as a bride decks herself with finery and jewels (18b) is a little grotesque, but it is
nothing if not expressive.   The cities of Judah shall be too
few and too small to contain all the returning exiles, even after
those who SWALLOWED UP Zion have departed (v. 19).   Here,
no more than in 18b, must we expect the Prophet's imagination to be controlled by logic or inhibited by concern about
problems of population.   Verse 20 is rather misleading in its AV
translation: it gives the impression that a newborn generation
is to take the place of those that are irretrievably lost.   This
was true enough, in a way, but the Prophet was not thinking of
generations past and present, but of the return of Jews who had
been scattered all over the world; render, therefore, with RV,
THE CHILDREN OF THY BEREAVEMENT SHALL YET SAY IN THINE
EARS, THE PLACE IS TOO STRAIT FOR ME: GIVE PLACE TO ME
THAT I MAY DWELL.   They would include the descendants of
the exiles from the Northern Kingdom (see on 43.5ff.) and
those who had gone to Egypt and elsewhere.   The passage
closes with a series of rhetorical questions which will arise in
the mind of the astonished and happy but bewildered mother.

It has already been noted that there is an element of poetic
hyperbole in the paragraph.   It may not be amiss to add that
it would be precarious to base upon v. 15 a doctrine of the
'motherhood' of God (cf. 66.13; Matt. 23.37).   Such exposi-
tions easily become bizarre and 'precious'.   What the Prophet
means is that the love of God is greater and more constant
than any human love, even of husband or mother.

14. The LORD . . . my Lord

Here 'Yahweh' and *adonai* (the ordinary word for 'lord') are
in parallel clauses.   For MY LORD read 'the Lord' (RV).   The
word is similar to English 'milord', in which the possessive
pronoun has become inseparably attached to the noun.

THE HEATHEN SHALL BRING ZION'S CHILDREN HOME
49.22-23

Yahweh has only to signal to the Gentiles (heathen nations) with his hand, and raise up a standard (cf. 5.26; 11.10) to the peoples (plural as RV,) and they will not only release his own but conduct them home with all ceremony. Infants shall be carried in breast-folds (RV 'bosom') and older children astride the shoulder. Kings and queens shall minister to their needs (cf. 60.16) and do them homage. The detail, LICK ('up' is rightly omitted in RV) THE DUST OF THY FEET (cf. Ps. 72.9) is not quite so objectionable as it may at first appear to us. It is parallel with THEY SHALL BOW DOWN TO THEE WITH THEIR FACES TO THE EARTH. Orientals are much more demonstrative than we when showing homage or affection. What is implied is that they shall kiss the feet of their one-time slaves, without noticing the dust which covers them.

THE TURNING OF THE TABLES
49.24-26

This passage contains a fine example of poetic inversion: literally:

> Shall the préy be táken *from the* míghty,
> Or the cáptives *of the* térrible *be* delívered?

> *The* cáptives *of the* míghty *shall be* táken,
> *And the* préy *of the* térrible *be* delívered.

Notice the skill with which the order of the words is varied as between question and answer. There is little doubt that LAWFUL CAPTIVE, lit. 'captive of the righteous' (v. 24), should read 'captives of the terrible'. This was the reading of LXX

and other versions (cf. RV marg.) and is now confirmed by
DSI. (The Hebrew words for 'righteous' and TERRIBLE look
much alike.) The word CONTEND is the same as 'strive' in
41.11 and has the force of 'go to law with'. The objectionable v. 26a, like 23b, is not quite so disgusting as may at first
appear. True, it was calculated to inflame Jewish chauvinism
in later eschatological pictures. What it means in this context
is that the panic-stricken Babylonians will be consumed by
internecine strife. Yet even though the passage has a strongly
nationalistic colouring, nationalism is not the last word, even
here. The section ends, as usual in DI, on the theocentric
note: ALL MANKIND SHALL KNOW THAT I AM YAHWEH THY
SAVIOUR, AND THY REDEEMER THE MIGHTY ONE OF JACOB.

XI

ISAIAH 50

ZION'S BANISHMENT IS NOT PERMANENT
50.1-3

The MOTHER in this passage is Zion, and those to whom it is addressed are individual Israelites, her children (cf. YOUR MOTHER). They supposed that their plight was due to one or the other of two causes: (1) either Yahweh had formally divorced their mother (cf. Deut. 24.1), or (2) he had sold them to some creditor (cf. Ex. 21.7; II Kings 4.1; Neh. 5.5,8; Matt. 18.25). Neither of these suppositions was right. Zion had indeed been unfaithful, but Yahweh had not given her any final bill of divorcement (read as RV in v. 1, 'wherewith I have put her away', for AV WHOM I HAVE PUT AWAY). As for creditors, what creditors could Yahweh have? The answers to the questions in v. 1 are 'Nowhere!' and 'No one!' The reason for the exile was his people's sins, not jealousy or whim or straitened circumstances on his part. The only thing that now stands in the way of their restoration is their own want of faith. When he sends his Prophet with a message of pardoning grace, he meets with no response (v. 2). This verse doubtless reflects the experience of the Prophet and is a good example of the way in which a 'word of the LORD' is also a word of the Prophet. Yahweh, whose power over nature is absolute, is fully capable of restoring the fortunes of his people (vv. 2b,3). Some think that the natural phenomena described in the passage refer to the original creation. This could suit 'at my rebuke I dry up the sea' (see on 51.9f.). Others think the reference is to the Exodus: this would equally suit the drying up of the sea (Ex. 14.21) and the stinking of the fish (cf. Ex. 7.18,21). There may be truth in both these views (see again on 51.9f.). On the other hand reference to phenomena which the Jews could actually witness in Babylonia should not be ruled out. The verbs in the passage are best rendered by present tenses, and v. 3 aptly describes sandstorms, which may darken the sky more completely than an eclipse of the sun.

2. their fish stinketh
LXX and DSI read 'are dried up'. As between this and 'stinketh' it is difficult to decide, in view of Ex. 7.18,21.

THE GETHSEMANE OF THE SERVANT
50.4-11

This is the third of the Servant songs. The word 'servant' nowhere occurs in it. The older commentators took the passage as autobiographical, embodying the experiences of the Prophet, and this view has been revived by those who think that the Servant is the Prophet himself. Even if the Servant is not the Prophet, the passage may nevertheless reflect the Prophet's experience; we have seen reason to believe that DI met with much opposition in the discharge of his task (cf. 45.9ff.; 46.8,12; 50.2).

The twice repeated LEARNED in v. 4 should be rendered 'disciples', as RV marg. The word is the same as in 8.16. 'Learned' people can be superior. What is meant is that the Servant is wakeful morning by morning to Yahweh's word, the word that enables him to sustain the weary (cf. RV). Yahweh has opened his ear, and he has responded with implicit obedience. Not only has he met with utter lack of sympathy; he has even been subjected to physical violence, scourgings, plucking out of the beard, and ignominious spitting. The text does not say whether this horse-play is from his own people or from the Gentiles. The close similarity of the maltreatment meted out to the Servant with that suffered by Jesus must strike every reader (see the marginal references). It should perhaps be pointed out that although the description reads as if it is of an individual, the terms in v. 6 could quite well be used of the sufferings of the nation Israel (cf. 1.5f.; Ps. 129.1ff.). The Servant expresses his confidence in the divine help (vv. 7ff.) and his determination to see his mission through to the end. The passage reads as if for the moment he is granted respite, though he must expect further trials. The language in vv. 8f. is forensic: JUSTIFIETH has the meaning of ' declare innocent ', ' acquit '; CONDEMN is to ' declare guilty '. Translate NEAR IS MY VINDICATOR, WHO WILL TAKE PROCEEDINGS AGAINST ME? LET US STAND UP TOGETHER (at the bar of judgement)! WHO IS MY ADVERSARY (i.e. the accuser or plantiff in my case)? LET HIM APPROACH UNTO ME! BEHOLD! THE LORD YAHWEH HIMSELF WILL HELP ME! WHO THEN CAN PROCURE A VERDICT AGAINST ME? There is no suggestion that the Servant is expecting his sufferings to culminate in death. On the contrary, THEY ALL SHALL WEAR OUT AS A GARMENT, MOTH SHALL CONSUME THEM!

In v. 10 both Yahweh and the Servant are referred to in the third person, and the address is to HIM (sing.) AMONG YOU (plur.) THAT FEARS YAHWEH. In v. 11 the address is to ALL YOU THAT KINDLE A FIRE, and the speaker is Yahweh. There is no real similarity between these verses and the preceding Song, nor any contact with the language and ideas of DI. They are generally thought to be from a later hand.

XII

ISAIAH 51

REMEMBER, AND FEAR NO MORE!
51.1-8

These verses consist of three short passages (vv. 1-3,4-6,7f.) beginning with HEARKEN UNTO ME! The introductory formula is slightly varied in v. 4, where RV renders 'Attend unto me!' The speaker in all the pieces is Yahweh, not the Prophet (cf. vv. 2,5,7).

The first passage is addressed to THOSE WHO FOLLOW AFTER RIGHTEOUSNESS . . . THAT SEEK YAHWEH (cf. v. 7), i.e. those who were sympathetic to the Prophet's message. They are exhorted to look to the rock whence they 'were' (so RV) hewn, and to the hole of the pit whence they 'were' digged. The rock from which they were quarried was Abraham their ancestor (cf. 41.8). The translation I CALLED HIM ALONE can be misleading, even though it is scriptural doctrine that Abraham alone was called; translate 'he was but one when I called him, and I blessed him and made him many' (cf. RV). The contrast is between the childlessness of Abraham at the time of his call and the promise to him of many descendants (cf. Gen. 15.5; see also on Isa. 44.1-5). The references to Abraham and Sarah may also be intended to remind the exiles of the mercies that attended the journey from Babylonian Ur to the promised land. The homeland shall be made hospitable for the reception of the returning exiles. The reference to EDEN . . . THE GARDEN OF YAHWEH may be reminiscent not only of the Eden story in Gen. 2 but also of the fabled paradise described in Ezek. 28.13; 31.8f.

3. shall comfort . . . will comfort . . . he will make
Hebrew literally 'hath comforted . . . hath comforted . . .
hath made', which is how RV translates it. The verb forms
are in what is called 'prophetic perfect' or 'perfect of certainty'. The subject is Yahweh, and what he intends to do is
already as good as *done*.

Verses 4-6 speak of LAW and JUDGMENT which are to be FOR
A LIGHT OF THE PEOPLES (i.e. Gentiles). The words are used
in the same special senses as in 42.1-4 (which see). The words
THE ISLES (coastlands) SHALL WAIT FOR ME are also reminiscent
of the first Servant Song (42.4), though here it is Yahweh, not
the Servant, for whom the nations shall wait. Some few MSS.
and one ancient version read 'peoples . . . nations' for MY
PEOPLE . . . MY NATION, making Gentiles, not Jews, the
recipients of the message. This is entirely in character with
the universalistic outlook of the passage. RIGHTEOUSNESS and
SALVATION have very nearly the sense of 'victory' and
'deliverance', as elsewhere in DI (see on 45.8; 46.13). Once
more, the appeal for trust and confidence is based upon the
creative power of Yahweh, who made heaven and earth, and
shall continue to be long after they have vanished away LIKE
SMOKE or like a WORN-OUT GARMENT (cf. II Pet. 3.10). Note
the RV marg. 'like gnats' for IN LIKE MANNER. This is a perfectly possible translation and would emphasize the evanes-
cence of all created life.

In vv. 7f. the summons to HEARKEN is once more addressed
to godly exiles, YE THAT KNOW RIGHTEOUSNESS, THE PEOPLE IN
WHOSE HEART IS MY LAW. The possessive pronoun MY with
LAW gives to LAW a less general content than in v. 4. It is here
the law that has been committed to the Jews as the outward
sign of their covenant with Yahweh. The figure of MOTH
eating a garment is repeated from v. 6 (cf. also 50.9) and well
expresses the brief triumph of those who reproach and revile
God's people.

THE REDEEMER-CREATOR
51.9-11

This is the first of three similar passages (the other two are
51.17-23; 52.1-6) beginning AWAKE, AWAKE! (cf. the 'Comfort
ye, comfort ye', of 40.1). The summons is addressed to 'the
arm of Yahweh' (cf. 40.10; 52.10; 53.1; Luke 1.51). The conception of Yahweh's arm as the instrument of deliverance and
judgement occurs frequently in Deuteronomy (cf. Deut. 4.34),
usually when recalling the Exodus from Egypt, 'with a mighty
hand, and with an outstretched arm'. The Exodus is clearly
in mind in the present passage, but the original reference of
four of the words in it, RAHAB, THE DRAGON, THE SEA, and THE
GREAT DEEP, is to the creation. Job. 9.13 (RV) speaks of 'the
helpers of Rahab'; in Job 26.12 (RV) Yahweh is said to
'smite through Rahab', which is parallel with 'the sea' (cf.
Ps. 89.9f.). The DRAGON (*tannin*) is a mythological personification of chaos in Job 7.12 (AV 'whale', RV 'sea-monster'),
Ps. 74.13; Isa. 27.1 (in all three passages associated with 'the
sea'). For (THE GREAT) DEEP (Hebrew *tehom*) see Gen. 1.2;
Prov. 8.27 (RV); Ps. 104.6. In Gen. 1.2 the word 'deep' is
without the definite article: 'darkness was upon the face of
deep (*tehom*)', almost as though 'deep' was a proper name, to
be spelt with a capital letter. The word is cognate with *Tiamat*,
the chaos-monster of Babylonian cosmogony. In fact, RAHAB,
THE DRAGON, THE SEA, and THE DEEP, are all synonyms for the
original chaos. The fullest form of the creation-myth is the
Babylonian, in which the god Marduk slew Tiamat, 'split her
like a flat-fish into two halves', and with one half made a
covering over the earth to keep the waters of the original chaos
from pouring in to flood the inhabited world. Hebrew cosmology presented much the same picture; cf. Gen. 1.6ff.; Ps.
104.6-9; Job 38.8-11. The Hebrews never liked the sea, partly,
no doubt, because there were no harbours on the coast of
Palestine to tempt them to maritime adventures, but mainly
because 'the sea' stood for all that is turbulent and chaotic.

always threatening to reduce the ordered world to the chaos from which it had been screened at the creation. This motif runs through the Bible, and when the seer in the Apocalypse says 'there was no more sea' (Rev. 21.1) he is thinking not so much of the sea that surrounds his island prison and separates him from his friends; what he means is that the danger that 'the sea' would overwhelm the world is finally removed.

The original reference in the passage is to the creation. But its primary reference is to the Exodus and the deliverance at the Red Sea: THAT MADE THE DEPTHS OF THE SEA A WAY FOR THE REDEEMED (RV) TO PASS OVER. RAHAB is another name for Egypt in Ps. 87.4 ('Rahab and Babylon', cf. RV marg.) and Isa. 30.7 ('Rahab that sitteth still', RV). What the Hebrews did was to take fragments from the old creation-myth, like so many shattered remnants of stained-glass, and use them to embellish the story of the Exodus. As it is some-times put, they 'historicized' the myth. Passages like the present, and Ps. 74.12-17, can refer equally well to the creation or to redemption. We might put it that for the Hebrews crea-tion is redemption, and redemption is creation. They extolled Yahweh as Redeemer-Creator, with the main emphasis upon his redeeming acts in history. They could never be content with 'natural religion'. That was the gravamen of the con-troversy between Yahweh and Baal. Baalism was pure naturalism. Yahwism, like Christianity, was rooted in his-tory. The Exodus in the O.T. had the same centrality for faith as the Resurrection has in the New.

Verse 11 is word for word the same as 35.10. Indeed, the whole of chap. 35 is Deutero-Isaianic in tone.

I AM YOUR COMFORTER: FEAR NOT!
51.12-16

This passage reads like a sequel to the preceding. To the cry AWAKE, AWAKE . . . O ARM OF YAHWEH . . . ART THOU

NOT IT . . . there comes the answer, I, EVEN I, AM HE! . . .
WHO ART THOU, THAT THOU ART AFRAID . . . ?   Yet the passage is full of perplexities. To whom is it addressed?   In
v. 12 YOU is masculine plural, THOU is feminine singular, and
in v. 13 the subject of the verbs FORGETTEST and HAST FEARED
(better RV 'hast forgotten' and 'fearest') is masculine
singular.   In these verses the address may be to the exiles,
thought of either as a community made up of individuals
(YOU), or personified as a woman (as in 41.14), or as a man
(41.8). Hebrew, it is true, can pass almost imperceptibly from
female to male personification; (e.g. in 41.14-16) which is nothing if not a unity, we have the feminine in 14, 15a and the
masculine in 15b,16.   The present passage is complicated by
the fact that v. 16 reads as if it is addressed to the Servant
(cf. 50.4; 49.2).   A study of the marginal references will show
that the passage as it stands is largely made up of quotations
from elsewhere in the prophecy; see also Jer. 31.35 for v.15.
Some scholars think that vv. 15f., which are only loosely
related to their context, are a conglomerate of quotations, based
upon Jer. 31.35 and the Servant Songs, and that they are a
later addition to the text.   And what is the logical connexion
between 16a and b: I HAVE PUT MY WORDS IN THY MOUTH . . .
THAT I MAY PLANT THE HEAVENS, AND LAY THE FOUNDATIONS OF
THE EARTH?   If we take the passage exactly as it stands, and
suppose that it comes from DI, we can only assume that he
judged it fitting to comfort his hearers with 'scriptural words'.
It seems more likely that the verses contain a genuine Deutero-
Isaianic nucleus, but that they have been heavily interpolated
(cf. on 42. 18-25).

12. a man that shall die
Better 'man that shall die' (RV), i.e. mortal man.

13. as if he were ready to destroy
Better 'when he maketh ready to destroy' (RV).
   14.   Literally, 'He that bends (i.e. under his burden, cf. RV
marg.) shall speedily be released, and he shall not die into the

pit, neither shall his bread fail'. The word for PIT generally
signifies the pit of death, the grave, Sheol. It can, however,
have a wider meaning, as of a pit for catching lions (cf. Ezek.
19.4,8). If a man was cast into such a pit, he could very
easily die. Jeremiah was in such a case (though the word
for 'dungeon' in Jer. 37.16 is not the same as here), and would
have starved if he had not been given a daily ration of bread
(Jer. 37.21). This may be the figure here. Some suppose that
the 'bent one' is DI himself, that he was put in prison and
later martyred (see note on the Suffering Servant, p. 32), and
that there is therefore a proper connexion between this verse
and v. 16. This, however, cannot be pressed, in view of the
'ragged' character of the passage.

ZION HAS DRUNK OF THE BOWL OF
STAGGERING LONG ENOUGH
51.17-23

The form of the Hebrew verb translated AWAKE, AWAKE! here
is more forcible than in v. 9 and 52.1, and conveys the suggestion that Zion can only rouse herself from her stupor by
a determined effort. She is pictured as having taken from
Yahweh's hand 'the goblet of reeling' (or 'staggering') and
drained it to the dregs: translate, WHICH HAST DRUNK AT THE
HAND OF YAHWEH THE CUP OF HIS WRATH; THE GOBLET OF REEL-
ING THOU HAST DRUNK AND DRAINED. For Yahweh's 'cup of
reeling' cf. Jer. 25.15ff. (RV); Ezek. 23.31ff.; Hab. 2.16; Lam.
4.21; Zech. 12.2; Rev. 14.10; 16.19. Most of the O.T. passages
date from the eve of the exile, and the figure well describes the
panic which must have come upon Jerusalem in the final
debacle. 'Reeling' denotes the unsteadiness which intoxication
produces before it passes into complete unconsciousness. Zion
has sunk into a state of utter hopelessness. In v. 18 we pass
from the second person THOU to the third person SHE. There is
no need to regard the verse as a later insertion. None of the
children Zion had borne and reared stretched out a hand to

steady her in her fall. It is not fanciful here to think of the
Prophet as making a distinction between what we should call
the ideal and the real, between Zion the mother and her
individual children. For THESE TWO THINGS (v. 19) cf. 47.9.
They are DESOLATION AND DESTRUCTION (of the city), and
FAMINE AND SWORD (the accompaniments of the siege), omit-
ting the commas after AV 'desolation' and 'famine'. For
BY WHOM SHALL I COMFORT THEE? read 'who shall comfort
thee?' with the major versions and DSI. This makes a perfect
parallel to WHO SHALL BE SORRY FOR THEE? for which a more
adequate translation is 'who shall bemoan thee?' (RV).
(Nowadays we say, 'I'm sorry!' to express light-hearted sympathy or apology). In v. 20 AT THE HEAD (RV 'top') OF ALL
THE STREETS makes a very long line, and is perhaps a gloss
from Lam. 2.19. For WILD BULL read 'antelope' (RV); cf.
Deut. 14.5, where the animal (again 'antelope' RV) is listed
with other harmless deer. For NET we should picture rather
a pit into which game animals were driven, breaking their
limbs in their terror. The promise of relief is introduced by
THEREFORE; the goblet of reeling shall be taken out of the
hand of Zion and given into the hand of those who have
afflicted her (cf. Jer. 25.17,26,28; Zech. 12.2; Rev. 16.19) and
treated her with such scorn that they have 'wiped their feet'
upon her prostrate body.

XIII

ISAIAH 52.1-12

PUT ON FESTAL GARMENTS, O ZION!
52.1-6

The opening words, AWAKE, AWAKE; PUT ON THY STRENGTH, recall 51.9, where the summons was to 'the arm of Yahweh'. DSI omits THY, which would make the summons word for word the same as there. There is not the suggestion conveyed by 51.17ff. (which see), that Zion has relapsed into stupor from which she can only by a supreme effort raise herself. The imperatives become bolder and more urgent as the time of release draws nearer (cf .vv. 7f., 11f.). Zion is to put on festal garments to meet her Lord (cf. Rev. 21.2). No more shall the uncircumcized and unclean enter the city (cf. Nah. 1.15), another parallel with Rev. 21.27; 22.14f. She had been prostrate in the dust, a fettered slave (51.23). Now she is to shake herself free and unloose the chains from her neck. The summons ARISE (*and*) SIT (*shebi*) reads rather oddly. If the text is right we must understand that Zion, having picked herself up from the dust, is to put on her festal robes and then seat herself in an attitude of composure. The addition of a single letter in the Hebrew would give the reading, 'Arise, O captive (*shebiyyah*) Jerusalem'. This is an exact verbal parallel to O CAPTIVE DAUGHTER OF ZION. The objection to it is that it is not good Hebrew style to have precisely the same words in parallel clauses.

In vv. 3-6 the personified DAUGHTER OF ZION gives place to YE . . . MY PEOPLE . . . THEM. Despite FOR THUS SAITH YAHWEH, linking them with vv. 1f. these verses are probably

not from DI. It was not the Prophet's teaching that the Jews
'were sold (so RV rightly, for YE HAVE SOLD YOURSELVES) for
nought'. The exile was the punishment for their sins (40.2;
43.27f.), and the texts to which reference is made in the margin
(45.13; 50.1) say nothing to the contrary. Verse 4, too, is hardly
relevant to the situation in the exile. It says, MY PEOPLE WENT
DOWN AT THE FIRST (RV) INTO EGYPT TO SOJOURN THERE—
meaning that they were guests in the country and should have
been treated as such—AND THE ASSYRIAN OPPRESSED THEM
WITHOUT CAUSE. Why the Assyrians, and no mention of the
Babylonians? The word HERE (v. 5) may point to Babylon.
But IN THAT DAY (v. 6), though the phrase is frequent enough
in eschatological prophecy (e.g. 7.18,20f.,23), is found nowhere
else in DI, who always speaks as if the fulfilment of his predictions is to be in the near future, not in some far beyond.
Notice, too, the four times repeated SAITH THE LORD, which
breaks up the passage into prose fragments.

5. they that rule over them make them to howl
Better, 'they that rule (tyrannize) over them do howl' (RV).
The text is not without difficulty, and a reading 'and their
(i.e. Israel's) rulers are profaned', has been suggested. This
makes a good parallel to MY NAME CONTINUALLY ALL THE DAY
IS BLASPHEMED (RV), and is now supported by DSI.

6. it is I
Better, 'here am I' (cf. RV marg.).

THE WORLD-KING ENTERS ZION
52.7-10

This is a passage of extraordinary animation and vividness.
Yahweh has achieved his victory over Babylon, and a messenger of good tidings approaches the holy city with the news
that the King is on his way, soon to make his entrance. For
a vivid background-picture cf. II Sam. 18.19-28. How beauti-

ful upon the mountains are the feet of this herald of good
tidings! (cf. Nah. 1.15). In Rom. 10.15 St. Paul refers the
passage to the preachers (plur.) of the Christian evangel; cf.
Isaac Watts, 'How beauteous are their feet'. The threefold
THAT PUBLISHETH PEACE, THAT BRINGETH GOOD TIDINGS OF
GOOD, THAT PUBLISHETH SALVATION suggests a picture of the
messenger at first descried upon a distant hill, then descend-
ing into the valley that separates it from one nearer the city,
reappearing and once more disappearing, until he comes within
earshot upon the nearest eminence and cries, THY GOD
REIGNETH! The cry is taken up by the watchmen on the
dilapidated walls (v. 8). Translate, HARK (cf. 40.3,6) THY
WATCHMEN! THEY LIFT UP THE VOICE, TOGETHER THEY BREAK
INTO A RINGING CRY OF JOY. The English phrase 'see eye to
eye' is a Hebraism taken from this passage, but the meaning it
has acquired, 'to agree', 'to think alike', is not quite that
of the original, which means 'to see close at hand' (cf. Num.
14.14 and RV marg.; Jer. 32.4). For WHEN THE LORD SHALL
BRING AGAIN ZION read 'when Yahweh returneth to Zion'
(cf. RV). Next (v. 9) even the ruins of Jerusalem are to
become alive and break forth into singing: for YAHWEH HATH
COMFORTED HIS PEOPLE, HE HATH REDEEMED JERUSALEM
(prophetic perfects). All this shall be witnessed by the
farthest ends of the earth. To make bare the arm was to draw
it out of the breast-fold as a preliminary to decisive action
(cf. 40.10; 51.9; Ps. 74.11). Nowhere does the combination
of nationalism and universalism so characteristic of DI come
to clearer expression than in this passage.

FROM BABYLON AWAY!
52.11-12

As so often in the most vivid passages in the prophecy, this
begins with a repeated DEPART YE, DEPART YE! (cf. 40.1;
51.9,17; 52.1). The word THENCE has sometimes been taken
as indicating that DI lived elsewhere than in Babylonia. This

is entirely out of keeping with the whole tenor of the prophecy; the word is explained if we think of the Prophet as himself already in imagination in Jerusalem (see the preceding section). The word for VESSELS has a wide latitude of meanings; the temple vessels, furniture in general, even weapons of war. The last of these meanings would be appropriate to an army on the march, and the returning exiles, as once the host in the wilderness, may be thought of so. But the injunction, BE YE CLEAN, YE THAT BEAR THE VESSELS OF YAHWEH, better applies to the priests who carry the sacred temple vessels which had been taken as booty by the Babylonians (cf. II Chron. 36.7; Ezra 1.7-11). The Prophet, however, may also have had in mind the ark (Num. 10.33ff.) and the tabernacle of the wilderness wanderings. In v. 12 the second Exodus is clearly set against the background of the first. Then the Israelites had departed out of Egypt IN HASTE (Ex. 12.11; Deut. 16.3; the word conveys a suggestion of trepidation or alarm, cf. II Sam. 4.4; II Kings 7.15). Not so this time. In the wilderness the Israelites had been led (Ex. 13.21f.) and, on occasion, protected (Ex. 14.19f.), by the pillar of cloud by day and the pillar of fire by night. This time Yahweh himself will be both vanguard and rearguard (cf. 58.8), guide and protector.

The passage is of interest as showing that the Prophet was not indifferent to what we call 'the externals of religion' (cf. also 52.1). He was concerned about the reverent handling of the temple vessels. Notwithstanding his critical attitude toward animal sacrifices (see on 43.22-28), he did not regard religion as pure disembodied spirit, without external observances. His enthusiasm for the rebuilding of the temple (44.28) shows that. Of all the prophets, Jeremiah comes nearest to saying that the externals of religion are of no importance (cf. Jer. 7.21ff.; 31.31-34). Yet even he spoke of a return to the homeland, with all that that implied for the re-institution of the temple cultus. 'The religious life needs more for its full culture than repentance and prayer. There is a place in it for common prayer, for disciplined observance, for a sacred place with hallowed associations. There is need for festival and ritual where soul quickens soul in mutual self-dedication, where the past helps the present to realize the life which has helped and guided all the generations. . . . If it was an exaggeration to make sacrifice an essential, it may be an equal exaggeration to demand its total abolition in the interests of purity of worship.' (A. C. Welch, *Jeremiah: his Time and his Work,* 1st ed., 1928, pp. 239f.).   In Christ, of course, the sacrificial system has been consummated and, in its original cruder forms, abolished (Heb. 8-10).   But Christianity, no less than Judaism, must have its cultic expressions (Heb. 10.25), its body as well as its soul.

XIV

ISAIAH 52.13-53.12

THE MAN OF SORROWS
52.13-53.12

This, the fourth and last Servant Song, is by common consent the most important, as it has always been the most discussed, passage in the O.T. The first thing to notice is that 52.13-15 is an integral part of the Song and should never be divorced from chap. 53. (The present chapter and verse divisions were no part of the original Bible.) The whole divides naturally into five paragraphs or strophes, corresponding to the paragraphs in the RV: (1) 52.13-15, The future exaltation of the Servant, (2) 53.1-3, The Man of Sorrows, (3) 53.4-6, His vicarious sufferings, (4) 53.7-9, His ignominious death, (5) 53.10-12, His resurrection and reward. Each of the first three Songs is put into the mouth of a single speaker, Yahweh in the first, the Servant in the second and third. Here the speaker in 52.13-15 and 53.11-12 must be Yahweh (cf. MY SERVANT). Who the speakers (WE) are in 53.1-10 is not indicated and is the most vigorously debated question arising out of the interpretation of the Song. In the present text of 53.8 the pronoun in MY PEOPLE must refer either to Yahweh or the Prophet, but there is reason to think that the text has suffered damage at that point (see the notes on the verse). The whole consists of the words of a human speaker or speakers, set in a framework of pronouncements by Yahweh.

The text of the passage is in places very difficult. This is due in part to the 'mysterious' character of the Song itself, and in part, it would seem, to textual corruptions. It may be that copyists found difficulty in understanding what they were transcribing and made matters worse by well-intentioned ' corrections '. Emendation on the basis of the versions can be hazardous, just because the passage was such a ' crux ' that they interpreted as well as translated it. We cannot, therefore, translate a version back into Hebrew and assume that this was the exact Hebrew which the translator had before him. The best plan seems to be to study the passage paragraph by paragraph and verse by verse, and gather up the problems in the note on ' The Suffering Servant ' (Introduction, pp. 29-36).

The reader is again recommended when reading the Servant Songs to follow up all the marginal references, and to discover others for himself. He will then see how their language is woven into the texture of N.T. thought. This is the more striking because it is not usual for the passages to be ' quoted ' at any length.

THE FUTURE EXALTATION OF THE SERVANT
52.13-15

13. Behold, my servant shall deal prudently
RV ' deal wisely ', RV marg. ' prosper '. This last is the right translation (as in Josh. 1.8, ' then thou shalt have good success ') and is a good parallel to what follows, HE SHALL BE EXALTED AND LIFTED UP, AND SHALL BE VERY HIGH (RV). The word has a variety of senses, beginning with ' act prudently '. The relation between this and ' prosper ' is that the prudent man is he who is likely to succeed.

14. As many were astonied at thee
' Astonied ' is hardly strong enough; ' appalled ' or ' awestruck ' would be more adequate. THEE is difficult, since nowhere else in the passage is the Servant addressed. Two of the versions read ' him ', probably rightly.

his visage was so marred more than any man, and his form more than the sons of men

These words are in parenthesis and are bracketed in RV. It is probable that they originally stood after 53.2. The meaning is not that the Servant was more marred than any (other) man but that he was so disfigured that he scarcely seemed human: cf. RV marg., 'from that of man, and his form from that of the sons of men'.

so shall he sprinkle many nations

The translation SPRINKLE is now generally abandoned. The verb SPRINKLE as a sacrificial term is never used with a direct accusative of object indicating a person or persons (as 'nations' here). It is always used of sprinkling *water* or *blood* upon someone or something (as in Lev. 5.9; 16.15; Num. 8.7). The rendering 'startle' (RV marg.) is based upon an Arabic word (not otherwise found in Heb.) meaning 'leap', hence 'cause to leap (in startled surprise)'. There is reason to think that the sentence is corrupt. Some such original as 'So shall many nations look upon him with amazement' has been suggested. This is based partly upon LXX, but there can be no certainty about it.

the kings shall shut their mouths at him

In dumb astonishment (cf. 49.7). AT HIM should go with the preceding clause as emended (see note there). THE is not in Hebrew.

consider

RV 'understand'. They shall come to 'discern the meaning' of what they had previously never even heard.

THE MAN OF SORROWS
53.1-3

1. Who hath believed our report?

The literal meaning of REPORT is 'something heard'. Translate, 'Who could have believed what we have heard?' (cf. RV marg.). What they have heard is something they would have supposed utterly incredible. As the passage is quoted in John 12.38; Rom. 10.16, it is the Prophet who laments that his hearers will not believe what he says. But in its original context here it is an exclamation of those who hear the evangel, who say in effect, 'This that we have heard is something we should have imagined impossible, and yet it is wondrously true!' Who are the speakers, the 'we' of vv. 1-6? There are three possibilities: (1) the Gentiles, (2) the Jews, (3) the Prophet speaking in the name of his fellow-countrymen. Those who think that the Servant is (collective) Israel naturally favour (1); those who think he was an individual or a godly nucleus of Israelites are in favour of (2) or (3). Recently, a few scholars who think the Servant is an individual have nevertheless admitted that the speakers are Gentiles. This is probably the correct view. If the Servant is Israel, 'we' *must* be the Gentiles; but it does not follow that if 'we' are the Gentiles, the Servant *must* be Israel. Whoever the Servant was, he had a mission to the Gentiles (42.1,4; 49.1,6). The end of chap. 52 pictures the Gentiles as dumb with amazement at what they see of the Servant. In 53.1-6 their silence gives place to speech. Unless they are the speakers here, they have no part in the drama. The most cogent objection to thinking of the 'we' as Gentiles is that it would put the sublimest thought in the O.T. upon the lips of heathen who are only just converted. But this would be almost equally true of the Jews at any period in their history. Actually, of course, the words are those of the Holy Spirit speaking through the Prophet.

the arm of the LORD
See on 51.9.

2. He shall grow up
The future tense is definitely wrong. Hebrew has 'and he grew up' (RV). Translate also, 'he *had* no form nor comeliness'. This is in accord with the tenses of the other verbs in

vv. 3-9, which even AV renders as past. The AV translators were probably influenced by the once universal view that the passage was Messianic prediction. The passage describes the sufferings and death of the Servant as having already taken place (though see below on 'he shall bear their iniquities', v. 11). This does not necessarily mean that he was already dead when the passage was written. As we have seen, the words of the 'we' are set in a framework of divine pronouncements which are in future tenses ('my servant shall prosper', etc.). The sufferings are therefore past in relation to an unspecified future. They may, or may not, have been past at the time the passage was written.

before him
If the translation is right, 'him' must refer to Yahweh (see v. 1). A better sense is obtained by rendering 'he grew (straight) up'. This may be explained by I Sam. 5.3f., where 'Dagon was fallen upon his face' is in the Hebrew 'fallen before him(self)', i.e. fallen straight forward.

3. He is despised and rejected of men
Or, 'Despised and forsaken of men'.

acquainted with grief
'familiar with (or, perhaps, "chastised by") sickness.'

HIS VICARIOUS SUFFERINGS
53.4-6

4f. Notice the emphatic pronouns, which are even more forcible in their Hebrew order. Literally:

> *Yet* ours *were the sicknesses that* he *carried,*
> *And* ours *the pains that* he *bore;*
> *Yet* we *supposed him stricken,*
> *Smitten of God, and afflicted.*

But he was pierced on account of our rebellions,
Crushed by reason of our iniquities;
The chastisement leading to our welfare was upon him,
And by means of his stripes there is healing for us.

The word STRICKEN has often been taken to mean that the
Servant was a leper; cf. Lev. 13.22,32, where 'plague' (of
leprosy) is literally 'a striking', and II Kings 15.5, where
Azariah is 'smitten' with leprosy (in both passages the words
are from the same root as 'stricken' here).   Although this
interpretation is as old as the early rabbis and the Vulgate, it
cannot be taken as certain.   It should, however, be noted that
the passage gives the impression that the Servant was subjected
to every conceivable pain and indignity: cf. 52.14; and 53.2,
which likens him to an unattractive and sickly plant.   There
is no evidence to show that this particular feature of the portrait was fulfilled in Jesus.

A careful comparison of vv. 3 and 4 will reveal poetic 'inver-
sions' similar to those in 49.24f.

In vv. 4-6 the idea of vicarious suffering is clearly present.

HIS IGNOMINIOUS DEATH
53.7-9

7. Render:

He was harshly treated, although he humbled himself,
And opened not his mouth.
As a sheep borne along to the slaughter,
And as a ewe before her shearers,
He was dumb,
And opened not his mouth.

Note the rhythmical incompleteness of the line, HE WAS DUMB.
This adds greatly to its forcefulness and pathos.   Also the
repeated, AND OPENED NOT HIS MOUTH, which has been

described as 'the most beautiful and expressive repetition in the whole prophecy'. HE IS BROUGHT AS A LAMB TO THE SLAUGHTER seems reminiscent of Jer. 11.19. Sacrificial animals were muzzled.

8. He was taken from prison and from judgment
This line is difficult, not because the text is corrupted but because the meaning of the Hebrew is obscure.   There are three possible translations: (1) the AV above, (2) 'By (reason of) oppression and judgement (i.e. an oppressive judgement, an example of "hendiadys", the use of two words to express a single idea) he was taken' (cf. RV), (3) 'Without hindrance and without judgement he was taken', i.e. no one made any attempt to secure for him a fair trial.   A modification of (1) is perhaps best: 'After arrest and sentence he was taken (off)', to execution.   The word 'taken' is ambiguous, since it can be understood in two different senses, as, indeed, it can be in English.   Some who think that the Servant was a leper (see note on v. 4) have argued that it means 'taken away (to God)', that the Servant died a natural death from leprosy, not the death of a felon.   They refer to Gen. 5.24 (Enoch); II Kings 2.3,5,10 (Elijah); Ps. 49.15; 73.24 (in the last two passages EVV translate 'receive').   But since the context refers to the Servant's 'grave' being made with the wicked, it must be assumed that he was executed after a judicial sentence.

and who shall declare his generation?
AV is here to be preferred to RV, 'and as for his generation, who *among them* considered that he was cut off out of the land of the living?' both on grammatical grounds and because in Hebrew poetry lines are 'end-stopped', i.e. the sense does not run on from one line into another, as it quite commonly does in English.   There is, however, good reason to think that the word rendered GENERATION could mean 'condition' or 'fortune'; cf. Ps. 24.6, which is better translated, 'This is the state (or lot) of them that seek after him'.   So here, 'Who gave a thought to his fate?'

for the transgression of my people was he stricken
MY is difficult. As the text stands it must refer either to
Yahweh or to the Prophet. If to Yahweh, there is nothing
in the near context to indicate that Yahweh is the speaker
(in v. 10 he is referred to in the third person). If it refers to
the Prophet: even assuming that it is the Prophet who is
speaking, he everywhere else identifies himself with the 'we'
for whom he speaks. The versions give no help, so that if
we are to emend the text it must be conjecturally. Probably
the original was 'for our rebellions' (cf. v. 5; and for 'rebellions' see on 43.25). LXX adds 'to death', probably rightly.

9. and he made his grave with the wicked
Lit. 'and one made' (with indefinite subject, cf. French *on
dit*). The meaning is 'and his grave was made', or 'and
they made his grave' (as RV).

and with the rich in his death
Christians have naturally understood this as an anticipation of
the burial of Jesus by Joseph of Arimathaea, 'a rich man . . .
in his own new tomb' (Matt. 27.57-60). In that case the first
member of the parallel, AND HIS GRAVE WAS MADE WITH THE
WICKED must not be pressed, since Jesus was not buried with
the malefactors. RICH men in O.T. times were often 'wicked',
as is witnessed by the denunciations of the prophets. But it is
questionable whether the words stand naturally in Hebrew
parallelism, as they have done in modern agitation. The
Hebrew reads awkwardly: literally, 'and with the rich in his
deaths' (plur.). Many scholars emend, with only slight change
in the Heb., to 'and with evil-doers his sepulchre'.

because he had done no violence
Better, 'although he had done . . .' (RV), as in Job 16.17
(RV), 'Although there is no violence in mine hands'.

HIS RESURRECTION AND REWARD
53.10-12

10. The text of this and the next verse is very difficult and uncertain. It is quite clear that the Servant is to live again and be fully rehabilitated. But there is no circumstantial description of his resurrection. The explanation may be that when the passage was written there was no clearly articulated doctrine of resurrection from the dead. The Prophet could therefore only express himself in general terms which led to mystification and consequent textual corruption. Another possibility is that the passage is reminiscent of the myth of the dying and rising god (Tammuz). In such 'mysteries' the revivification of the god is assumed but never described.

Yet it pleased the LORD to bruise him; he hath put him to grief
The Hebrew consonantal text reads literally: 'But Yahweh was pleased to crush him the sickness.' The Vulgate has 'The Lord was pleased to crush him with sickness', and the LXX 'The Lord was pleased to cleanse him from sickness'. The explanation of the difference between the two versions lies in the fact that the same consonants which mean 'crush' in Hebrew mean 'cleanse' in Aramaic. The objection to 'cleanse' here is that nowhere else in the O.T. is the word used in its Aramaic meaning, and that it has already been used in the sense 'crush' in v. 5. On the whole it seems best to translate as the Vulgate does. DSI has the remarkable reading, 'But Yahweh was pleased to crush him and he pierced him' (cf. v. 5). This *may* be the right reading.

when thou shalt make his soul an offering for sin etc.
To whom does THOU refer? An equally good translation is, 'when his soul (i.e. he) makes an offering for sin'. The objection to both the EVV, and indeed to the Hebrew text as it stands, is that the line is not 'end-stopped' (see on v. 8

above).   The deletion of a single letter ('jot', the smallest letter
in the Hebrew alphabet, Matt. 5.18) and a slight rearrangement
of the word divisions, would give the meaning, 'Truly he gave
himself as an offering for sin'.   This would be a good parallel
to 'Yahweh was pleased to crush him with sickness' of the
preceding line, but there is no certainty that it was the original
reading.   The word for 'offering for sin' (*asham*) means
properly 'guilt-offering', for which see Lev. 5.14-6.7; 7.1-7;
in the RV (AV has 'trespass offering ').

he shall see HIS seed, he shall prolong his days
An alternative translation is 'he shall see seed that prolongs
days', and this on the whole is to be preferred.   Exactly what
is intended by SEED it is difficult to say.   Those who think that
the Servant is Israel naturally think of the survival and world-
mission of the nation, and of the SEED as individual Israelites
or even Gentile proselytes.   Those who think he was an
historical individual think of his return to life on this earth;
this is consistent with either physical (cf. Job 42.16) or spiritual
seed.   Those who think the Servant is the Messiah (Christ)
naturally think of spiritual rather than physical seed.   The text
is consistent with any of these views and does not enable us
to decide between them.   The view any reader takes will
depend upon his conclusion as to who the Servant was.

pleasure
'purpose' (see on 44.28).
   11.   The literal rendering of the (unpunctuated) Hebrew is:
'From the travail of his soul he shall see he shall be satisfied
by his knowledge a righteous one my servant shall justify the
many and their iniquities he shall bear.'   The LXX reads
'light' after 'see'.   This reading is now confirmed by both
the Dead Sea Isaiah scrolls and may be taken as firmly established.   The words 'light' (*'or*) 'see' (*yir'eh*) look and
sound rather alike, and one of them could easily be omitted
by a copyist.   The word 'a righteous one' (*saddik*) is metrically
redundant and difficult to construe grammatically, and looks

very like a distorted repetition of 'shall justify' (*yasdik*). The addition of the one word ('light') and the deletion of the other ('a righteous one'), with some rearrangement of the punctuation (which was no part of the original text), would give this reading:

> *After his travail of soul he shall see light;*
> *He shall be satisfied with his knowledge.*
> *My servant shall justify many,*
> *And he shall bear their iniquities.*

The tense of the last line should be noted; it is future. Verse 4 has 'he bore', the same verb but in the past tense. As we have seen, the sufferings described in vv. 1-6 are *past*, but past *from a future standpoint*. The reading HE SHALL BEAR here may indicate that the sufferings of the Servant were in reality thought of as future.

12.   Therefore will I divide him a portion with the great, and he shall divide the spoil with the strong

An equally good translation is: 'Therefore I will give him the many for his portion, and numerous shall be his spoil.' According to the usual translation, the Servant is to take his share of spoil with the GREAT and STRONG. The alternative translation offered makes them his SPOIL, the reward for his sacrifice. Nor does SPOIL necessarily indicate a military conqueror. It is found in 9.3 in parallelism with harvest rejoicing (cf. Prov. 31.11). The word 'great' in the EVV is the same as 'many' in 52.14f.; 53.11, and again at the end of this verse. Consistency requires that it should be rendered 'many' here. The word 'strong', with which it is parallel, properly means 'numerous'; so in Prov. 7.26; where again the words are in parallelism, and of which the literal translation is, 'For she hath cast down many wounded, and numerous are all her slain' (AV 'many strong *men*', RV 'a mighty host', both try to express number *and* strength). Twice at the beginning, and three times at the end of the Song, the 'one' Saviour stands

over against the 'many'. It seems certain that Jesus had this
passage in mind when he said that he came 'to give his life
a ransom for many' (Mark 10.45).

and made intercession for the transgressors
Lit. 'and for the rebellious ones he interposed', i.e. he came
between them and the punishment they deserved. Here again,
and in the last clause but one, HE BARE THE SIN OF MANY, the
thought of vicarious suffering is clearly expressed.

XV

ISAIAH 54

THE INCREASE OF ZION'S CHILDREN
54.1-10

The theme of this passage is similar to that of 44.1-5; 49.14-21; 50.1; 51.1-3; but the thought is upon the natural increase of Zion's children *in*, rather than upon the return of her exiled children *to*, the homeland. Zion, the childless wife, is to break forth into singing because she is to be a fruitful mother. Verse 1 is quoted by St. Paul in Gal. 4.27, but allegorically of the heavenly and earthly Jerusalem; a striking example of the way in which the N.T. sometimes reinterprets the Old. THE DESOLATE is a figure for Jerusalem during the exile; THE MAR-RIED WIFE is the city before the exile. In v. 2 the figure changes to that of a nomad tent-dweller who must enlarge her tent and therefore lengthen the ropes and strengthen the stakes that keep it erect. Zion's population (v. 3) shall spread (RV) outwards (cf. Gen. 28.14) to her desolated daughter cities which during the exile had been occupied by peoples (GENTILES AV, 'nations' RV) like the Edomites (cf. Ezek. 35.1-10). The re-occupation shall be effected peacefully. Once more Zion is bidden to FEAR NOT! (41.10,13f; 43.1,5; 44.2). She shall forget the shame of her youth before the exile, and remember no more the reproach of her widowhood in exile (v. 4). Her husband is none other than her Maker, Yahweh of Hosts, the Holy One of Israel her Redeemer, the God of the whole earth (v. 5). That should be assurance enough. Verse 6 will bear a more vivid translation: FOR AS A WIFE (SO RV) FORSAKEN AND GRIEVED IN SPIRIT YAHWEH CALLED THEE; AND A WIFE OF

142

YOUTH, THAT SHE SHOULD (ever) BE FORSAKEN! SAITH THY GOD.
The answer implied is 'Never! Impossible!' If for a little
while Yahweh forsook her, now he will gather her with great
mercies (v. 7). In OVERFLOWING (so RV rightly, see below) or
'a flood of' wrath Yahweh hid his face for a moment, but with
everlasting 'devotion' he, her Redeemer, will have mercy upon
her. The word 'devotion' (EVV 'kindness'), Hebrew *hesed*,
is one of the most beautiful words in the language, and
expresses the emotional tie which binds the parties to a
covenant to one another. Verses 6-8 almost convey the suggestion that Yahweh regrets that he had to treat his people
so severely (cf. Jer. 31.20). This thought is continued in vv.
9f. if we read them, as we must, in the light of Gen. 8.21f.;
9.14ff. Before the Flood Yahweh 'repented' (Gen. 6.6) that
he had made man; after it his feelings were tinged with regret.
Such anthropomorphisms need not occasion any misgivings;
they even add to the appeal of Scripture. God, in the Bible,
is never heartless or unfeeling, as a pure transcendental monotheism could so easily represent him. The literal translation
of the opening words of v. 9 is as in RV marg.: THIS IS UNTO
ME AS THE DAYS OF NOAH. The words for DAYS and WATERS
are spelt almost exactly the same, and it matters little which
we read here, the more so since THE WATERS OF NOAH occurs
later in the verse. THIS refers to the time of exile. The
passage closes with the assurance that Yahweh's *hesed*, and
his COVENANT OF PEACE, which is its guarantee, are more enduring than even the mountains and hills.

> *This, this is the God we adore,*
> *Our faithful, unchangeable Friend;*
> *Whose love is as great as His power,*
> *And neither knows measure nor end.*

2. let them stretch forth

A slight textual change to the imperative 'stretch forth' would
give a more natural reading, and this is supported by the
versions.

8. In a little wrath
The Hebrew word for 'a little' is meaningless and occurs
nowhere else. A change of a single letter to one of related
sound would give 'overflowing' (so RV). The AV 'a little'
for the meaningless word was probably influenced by 'small'
in the previous verse.

THE NEW JERUSALEM
54.11-17

This passage begins abruptly, without any introductory
formula. It is a passage of quite remarkable interest. It is
obviously the original of the description of the New Jerusalem
in Rev. 21f. (see especially 21.18-21). Equally obviously, the
picture of the city adorned with precious stones goes back to
stories of a mythological paradise in the primeval past, of which
a description is still extant in Ezek. 28.13f. (cf. also Gen.
2.11f.). In other words, this paragraph is a link between the
mythological paradise in the primeval past and the equally
mythological (see Introduction, p. 27) paradise of the age to
come. The first paradise in the Bible is a garden, the last is a
city (Rev. 21.2). 'God made the country, man made the
town' has become almost a proverb. But it is not the final
word. When the sun shines through the morning haze on the
sky-scrapers of New York, it can light them up with a glory
that is almost ethereal. But New York is not the New Jerusalem. Man was cast out of the first Eden and the way back to
it is guarded by the Cherubim with their swords of whirling
flame (Gen. 3.24). He cannot recover his lost innocence.
Meanwhile he builds his cities. The man of faith looks for
'the city which hath the foundations, whose architect and
maker is God' (Heb. 11.10, RV marg.). 'The tree of life'
of which man once desired to eat (Gen. 2.9; 3.22) and to
which he was denied access, has been transplanted thither
(Rev. 2.7; 22.2,14), and its leaves are for the healing of
the nations. The Gospel is set for the redemption of the

whole of human life and activity.   God will save even the
city.

11. I will lay thy foundations with fair colours
Lit. 'I will set thy stones in antimony' (RV marg.).   'Antimony' or 'stibium' was a black mineral powder, used by
women to give more brilliance to their eyes by darkening the
edges of the eyelids.   The only O.T. parallel to the figure of
antimony in building is I Chron. 29.2, where 'glistening stones'
(RV 'stones for inlaid work') is literally 'stones of (i.e. set in)
antimony'.   The figure of Zion, Yahweh's bride, 'made up'
with antimony (cf. II Kings 9.30, Jezebel! Jer. 4.30) is so daring, even in an architectural context, that it is not surprising
that attempts have been made to emend the text.   A comparatively slight change would give a precious stone meaning perhaps 'rubies' or 'carbuncles' (the word translated
'emerald(s)' in Ezek. 27.16; 28.13, and in the description of
the high priest's breastplate, Exod. 28.18; 39.11).   This receives
some support from LXX and from 'sapphires' in the following parallel clause.   It may be, however, that the LXX shrank
from the suggestion of 'sex-appeal' in the Hebrew.   Sex
metaphors can be carried to extravagant lengths by mystical
writers.   The O.T. attitude to sex is frank and healthy.   The
Bible is never prudish.

12. windows
Better 'pinnacles' or 'battlements', as in Ps. 84.11, where the
meaning is 'a battlement and shield'.

agates
The Hebrew denotes some kind of sparkling stone, 'rubies' in
RV here and Ezek. 27.16.   A study of the passages referred
to in the notes on this section, together with their marginal
alternatives, will indicate that it is often impossible to know
precisely what precious stones are referred to.

  13.   The logic of this is that there shall be no need of priests,
prophets, teachers of any kind! cf. Jer. 31.34.   Notice that

CHILDREN . . . CHILDREN occurs in parallelism. This is
unusual. The word (*banayik*) can be pointed to mean
'builders' (*bonayik*). The objection to the change is that in
vv. 11f. it is Yahweh who is to build the city.

15. gather together
Better 'stir up strife'.

for thy sake
'because of thee' (RV). The rendering 'shall fall away to
thee' (RV marg.) may be disregarded.
   17. A prophecy many times fulfilled. The country that
encourages anti-Semitism invites disaster.

XVI

ISAIAH 55

'COME; FOR ALL THINGS ARE NOW READY'
55.1-5

This passage is the O.T. counterpart of the parable of the Great Supper (Luke 14.15-24). To understand it we should remember that in the East water is still sold in the streets, and that a man wishing to be generous will buy up the stock of a water-carrier or baker and order him to distribute it gratis. The word BUY in v. 1 has the specific meaning 'buy corn'. The text seems overloaded and should perhaps be shortened to: HO, EVERY ONE THAT THIRSTETH, COME YE TO THE WATERS, AND LET HIM THAT HATH NO MONEY COME; BUY CORN AND EAT, YEA WINE AND MILK WITHOUT MONEY AND WITHOUT PRICE. The largesse of the divine Donor goes beyond the necessities of water and bread to include the luxuries of wine and milk. All are symbols of the true bread, THAT WHICH IS GOOD, the bread of heaven (cf. John 6.27,32), as contrasted with the bread which perishes and for which men expend toil and money. There is no emphasis in YOUR SOUL upon the soul as distinct from the body (cf. on 42.1): the meaning is only DELIGHT YOURSELVES IN FATNESS. FATNESS may be used of spiritual food; cf. 'They shall be abundantly satisfied with the fatness of thy house' (Ps. 36.8). The metaphor is in accord with the oriental taste for plenty of oil in cooking. The sum of the matter is that Yahweh offers spiritual food gratis. This is Old as well as N.T. doctrine.

In vv. 1-3a the language can be read as that of the Prophet

147

only. We can visualize him proclaiming it in the bazaar in the name of the Lord who has commissioned him. But it is quite impossible to disjoin vv. 1-3a from 3b-5, in which it is plainly Yahweh who speaks. This implies that vv. 1-3a are the words of Yahweh as well. The whole is a striking example of the way in which a prophet could not only speak *on behalf of* but even *as* God (a similar passage is 5.1-7). The word of the prophet *is* the word of God, his indignation God's indignation, his sorrow God's sorrow. It is pre-eminently in this that we have in the O.T. anticipations of the Incarnation, of the Word become flesh.

Opinion is sharply divided on the interpretation of vv. 3b-5. Is the meaning that there is to be revival of the Davidic monarchy? Or is it that THE SURE MERCIES OF DAVID are now to be transferred to the nation? Between these views it is extremely difficult to decide. Acceptance of the former would imply that the Prophet's expectations of Cyrus had faded, as they may well have done, and that a new Messianism took their place in his mind. On the whole, the second view is to be preferred: THE EVERLASTING COVENANT is to be made with YOU (plural), i.e. the Jewish people. Notice once more the association of the COVENANT with MERCIES (plur. of *hesed*, see on 54.8 above, where the word is rendered 'kindness'). For the covenant with David and its consequent mercies see II Sam. 23.5; Ps. 18.50; 89.28; all of which go back in nucleus to II Sam: 7.8-16. By EVERLASTING COVENANT is not meant a covenant which begins now and lasts for ever, but a lasting covenant which is also grounded in the past. Even if the meaning of the passage is that the Davidic monarchy is to be restored, the emphasis is upon spiritual rather than political or imperialistic leadership. WITNESS (v. 4) is used in 43.10; 44.8 of the spiritual calling of Israel. Nor should any undue emphasis upon political leadership be read into the words LEADER AND COMMANDER, both of which particular Hebrew words suggest moral rather than military leadership. On the view that the Prophet was thinking of the restoration of the Davidic monarchy, v. 5, with its change from the plural YOU

to the singular THOU, is difficult. It is hard, notwithstanding
Ps. 18.43, to imagine that the future king is addressed as if he
were already present, and more natural to take the address as
to Israel. The word NATIONS is singular in the Hebrew (RV 'a
nation'). It is to be understood in the general sense of
'people' (see on 49.7-13). Again, the emphasis is upon moral
and spiritual leadership, whether of the Davidic king or of the
nation. Even if DI thought of a Messiah (apart from Cyrus
'my anointed one', in 45.1), he was no perfervid nationalist.

DO NOT DELAY!
55.6-13

This well-known passage needs little comment. The suggestion in SEEK YE THE LORD WHILE HE MAY BE FOUND is that
delay may be fatal. Divine grace is no excuse for human
complacency (Ps. 95.7f. RV; Rom. 6.1.f.; Heb. 3.7-19). Let
the wicked forsake his way and return to the God of all
pardon, whose thoughts and ways are as much higher than
man's as the heavens are higher than the earth. That Yahweh's
word will not fail to accomplish his purpose is as sure as that
the rain from heaven will cause earth's seed to germinate.
Verses 10,11a, again, might be taken as an independent utterance of the Prophet; 11b shows that it is both his and
Yahweh's. It is a humbling and heart-searching thought for
a preacher that the word which he utters is, or should be, the
very word of God! The preacher should strive to be in the
goodly fellowship of the prophets.

In the concluding verses (12f.) the Prophet returns to the
theme of the second Exodus through the transformed wilderness (41.18f.; 43.18ff.). It might be supposed that once the
exiles had completed their journey the way would revert to
its former wilderness condition; the Jews were not to dwell
there permanently. But no! it is to remain TO YAHWEH FOR
A NAME, FOR AN EVERLASTING SIGN. For NAME in the sense of
a 'memorial' cf. 56.5 (RV), 'a memorial and a name', II Sam.

18.18; and for SIGN with the meaning 'monument' or 'inscription', Isa. 19.19f. We may render, 'and it shall be to Yahweh for a memorial, for an everlasting inscription which shall never be effaced'. The transformed wilderness will be preserved in perpetuity as a commemorative park! If anything could show that the Prophet looked for a lasting transformation of nature, it is this closing verse. Even if he was mistaken in that particular, the Word of God of which he was the evangelist and herald shall assuredly abide for ever.

APPENDIX

On 40.6 (p. 40)
The Hebrew word (*hesed*) translated GOODLINESS in the AV,
'beauty' in RSV, almost certainly means here 'constancy',
'loyalty', 'devotion'. It is the word used in Hos. 6.4., where
'constancy' is surely the meaning (AV 'goodness', RSV
'love').

The emendation 'And I said' is dubious, notwithstanding
now the RSV. The Hebrew is literally 'A voice says, "Cry"'',
and 'he (i.e. one, indefinite subject) says', and the construction
is exactly as in 6.3. The meaning is something like 'and
answer comes back'. The Prophet hears two voices, the one
replying to the other. The words ALL FLESH IS GRASS are the
first speaker's answer to the question WHAT SHALL I CRY?
The voices are antiphonal, again as in 6.3.

On 40.19f. (pp. 45f.)
The two Hebrew words translated HE THAT IS SO IMPOVER-
ISHED THAT HE HATH NO OBLATION are unintelligible. They
break up the metre, are omitted by the Vulgate, and are
probably a later insertion. The first of them, according to
Jerome, was a kind of wood (mulberry?), an explanatory gloss
on 'tree' following. In that case the description is not of two
images, one for the rich and the other for a poor man, but
of one imposing image, like that of Nebuchadrezzar (Dan. 3).
The verses are an answer to the question in v. 18 and may be
translated:

> An idol? A craftsman casts it,
>> and a goldsmith overlays it with gold,
>> and casts silver chains.
> They (indefinite subject) choose a durable wood,
>> and look for a joiner skilled to work it (the wood),
>> to secure the image so that it will not fall down.

The SILVER CHAINS were chain-fencing, intended to rail off the image (cf. I Kings 6.21), rather like a 1914-18 war memorial. Ch. 41.6f., which according to many should follow 40.19f. (see p. 45), should remain where it stands in ch. 41. It is too farcical in the context of 40.19f.

On 41.6f. (p. 52)
See note immediately above. The implication is that the idolaters try to overcome their fears by arming themselves with more potent 'gods', much as we do today.

On 41.10 (p. 53)
It is now known from a Ras Shamra text that the verb translated BE NOT DISMAYED means 'to be afraid', an exact parallel to the preceding FEAR.

On 43.22-28 (pp. 76f.)
The pronoun ME in v. 22 stands before the verb that governs it, and is most emphatic: 'But (it was) not me you called . . . !' Then the verb 'call' can have the meaning 'invite' (so in I Kings 1.9f., cf. RSV). The meaning is therefore 'Do not suppose that it was me you invited (to your festal sacrifices), or that you went to the length of wearying yourself on my account.' Sacrifices in pre-exilic times were occasions for jollification, often gluttony (cf. Amos 4.4f.; 5.21f.; 6.4), since most of the flesh of the so-called 'peace-offering' or 'sacrifice' was eaten by the worshippers themselves. In any case 'calling upon (or invoking) Yahweh' was usually accompanied by a sacrifice (cf. Ps. 116.17). To whom, then, were the sacrifices offered, if not to Yahweh? The declared intention was to offer them to Yahweh, but Yahweh implies that in reality they were not offered to him, but to some 'strange (i.e. foreign) god' (cf. 43.12; Ps. 44.20; 81.9).

On 44.21 (p. 84)
For THOU SHALT NOT BE FORGOTTEN OF ME, which is very dubious in the Hebrew, since a verb in the passive voice does

not take an accusative object, read 'you must not play false with me'. The slight change in the Hebrew was suggested in 1939, and is now supported by DSI. The verb is that used by Eve ('beguiled') of the serpent in Gen. 3.13.

On 44.23 (p. 85)

The verb 'glorify himself' is not from the usual root 'glory', 'glorify' (*kbd*), but is related to two nouns which denote some kind of festive garment or head-dress (e.g. in 61.10 of a bridegroom's 'garland'). The probable meaning is that Yahweh 'puts on' Israel as a garland or crown, i.e. he 'points to (the redeemed) Israel as his crowning achievement'. There is much in the prophecy to suggest this: Yahweh created Israel for his 'glory' (*kābōd*), 43.7.

On 45.9 (p. 90)

THY WORK is, in the Hebrew, one word. If we detach the pronoun suffix THY from its noun, the letter (*k*) can be read as a conjunction (*kī*, 'that'). The sense will then be 'or (the finished) work (say) that he (the potter) has no skill'.

On 45.10 (p. 90)

The meaning is not 'a (i.e. any) father . . . or mother' (AV 'woman'), but HIS (own) FATHER . . . or mother'; so AV, which supplies the possessive pronoun *his,* though it is not in the Hebrew (*contra* RV and RSV).

On 45.14 (p. 91)

On second thoughts I am fairly confident that it is not to Cyrus that the Africans are to COME OVER, but to Zion-Jerusalem. The verb COME (literally 'pass') OVER is used of making a pilgrimage in Amos 5.5; Ps. 42.4. The CHAINS are not leg-fetters, which would make the journey impossible, but manacles or hand-cuffs (cf. Jer. 40.4) which the pilgrims as they approached Jerusalem would fasten on themselves as evidence that they were not coming with any hostile intent.

On 45.24 (p. 94)
Translate 'Only in Yahweh'—it shall be said—'is there victory and might'. This is supported by DSI and by Arabic idiom.

On 47.3 (p. 99)
Translate 'I will parley with no man' (cf. RV margin 'make truce with'). Verse 4 is probably a later addition. It speaks of OUR REDEEMER, whereas in the rest of the chapter the speaker is Yahweh himself.

On 49.4 (p. 109)
my judgment (RSV 'right') **is with Yahweh.**

The word JUDGMENT (*mishpāt*) is used here in its ordinary sense of a decision or verdict pronounced by a judge. The suffix **my** can mean either 'the judgment passed by me' (subjective genitive) or 'the judgment which Yahweh will pass on me' (objective genitive). The latter is intended here. In the light of the second half of the verse, 'my recompense (RSV) is (safe) with my God', the Servant is expressing his conviction that Yahweh will give a favourable verdict on his work, that God will affirm his confidence in him.

On 52.14 (pp. 131f.)
As many were astonied at thee
'Horrified' is not too strong for the Hebrew verb. The pronoun THEE may be rendered 'him' without altering the text. Hebrew can sometimes change from one personal pronoun to another without intending any actual change of person (e.g. at 61.7, RSV).

His visage was so marred . . .
There is no need to read the lines 'his appearance was unlike that of a man, so disfigured that he scarcely seemed human' after 53.2 (see the next note).

So shall he sprinkle many nations

The verb SPRINKLE is in the singular number and stands before MANY NATIONS, which of course is in the plural. But examples are not wanting in Hebrew where a subject in the *plural* is preceded by its verb in the *singular*. Such examples cannot of course be detected in an English translation, but those who read Hebrew may consult the RSV at 13.22, 'Hyenas (plural) will cry' (singular), to cite only one passage. In 1942 a Swedish scholar, H. S. Nyberg, suggested that the correct translation should be 'so shall many nations sprinkle upon him': 'upon', the 'pilot' preposition to the verb 'sprinkle' (see the note on p. 132) is actually in the Hebrew text here, though in the EVV it is construed with the second half of the line ('at him' in AV and RV, 'because of him' in RSV and RV margin). So far as I know, no British scholar has adopted Nyberg's suggestion (few of them have ever come across it), but I am strongly of the opinion that it is on the right lines. (For my reasons and the reference to Nyberg's work see *The Second Isaiah*, pp. 228f.) What the nations are to sprinkle on the Servant is not stated, but it would be either blood or water, and the purpose of the sprinkling would be to decontaminate, or disinfect, and so cleanse the Servant (cf. Lev. 14.7, 51; 16.19; Num. 19.4). After all, he looks 'horrible', and the nations would be likely to treat him as they would a leper, whether or not he was one (see note on p. 135).

kings shall shut their mouths at him

Probably again to avoid being contaminated by him. They would be highly superstitious. For such decontamination rituals see J. G. Frazer, *The Golden Bough, Part II, Taboo and the Perils of the Soul*, London, 1922.

If the above suggestions are right, the words of v. 14, 'his appearance was unlike that of a man, so disfigured that he scarcely seemed human'—they are bracketed in the RV and in parentheses in the RSV—may stay where they are. They explain why the MANY NATIONS act as they do.

On 53.8 (p. 137)
for the transgression of my people was he stricken
The Hebrew is literally 'for the transgression of my people a
stroke (or striking) to them'. The last word 'to them' is—to
give the Hebrew letters—*lmw*. For it the LXX, which is
accepted by most scholars and recommended in the first
edition of this Commentary, reads *lmwt* (pointing *lammāweth*,
'to death'). The EVV 'he was stricken' understand the last
word *lmw* (pointed *lāmō*) as 'to him'. But the great majority
of scholars are agreed that 'to them' (plural) is the only possible meaning. That is why they prefer the LXX reading 'to
death'. As explained on p. 137, the possessive pronoun in
MY PEOPLE (Hebrew *'ammī*) is difficult, since it cannot very
well refer either to Yahweh or to the Prophet. But a simple
change of vowel from *'ammī* to *'ammē* provides a possible
solution. It involves no alteration of the standard Massoretic
text, which consists of consonants only. The vowel points were
added later by Jewish scribes (the so-called Massoretes) well
on in the Christian era, and scholars have no hesitation in
altering vowels if by so doing they can get a more intelligible
meaning. If, then, we read *'ammē* for *'ammī*, a literal translation of the Hebrew is 'for the transgression of peoples of a
striking to them'. The expression 'peoples of a striking'
means 'peoples who deserve to be stricken' (cf. RV margin
'to whom the stroke was due'). This is supported by I Kings
2.26, 'thou art worthy of death', i.e. 'you deserve to die',
where the Hebrew is literally 'you are a man of death'. The
meaning will then be 'for the transgression of peoples who
deserved to be stricken themselves'. This gives a sense which
is in entire harmony with the context, and at the same time
involves no alteration of the Massoretic text.

and with the rich
On p. 137 the conjectural emendation 'with evil-doers' is
recommended. But some years ago a suggestion was made that
the Hebrew word RICH (*'āshīr*) is cognate with an Arabic
word (*guthr^{un}*) meaning 'rabble' or 'dregs of mankind'. This

is probably to be accepted, and we have two parallel lines, 'They buried him among felons, and with the dregs of men when he died', with no alteration of the Massoretic text.

On 53.10 (p. 138)

Yet it pleased the LORD to bruise him, he hath put him to grief
The English word *bruise* used to mean 'break', 'crush', and that is its meaning here, notwithstanding John 19.36. (It should be said that Isa. 53 is not a prophecy *in detail* of the passion of our Lord. For example, Jesus was not buried in a felon's grave.) In current English a bruise is a blow which discolours the skin but does not break any bones.

The words HE HATH PUT HIM TO GRIEF are only one short word in the Hebrew. It is pointed as a verb, but it can equally well be pointed as a noun 'sickness'.

The rendering of the Vulgate, 'The LORD was pleased (or 'It was the LORD's purpose', see on the word 'pleasure' on p. 139) to crush him with sickness' is a perfectly good translation of the Hebrew. There is an exact parallel to the construction in Mal. 3.24, 'I will smite the earth a curse', i.e. with a curse, a kind of Latin ablative, though such a construction in Hebrew is called an instrumental accusative. Hebrew has no ablative but instead uses nouns in various accusative relations to a verb.

The sense of the first part of v. 10 may be given as 'It was in the purpose of the LORD that he should be broken by suffering.' If this seems to us morally objectionable, we should reflect that the salvation of mankind—human nature being what it is—can hardly be accomplished without suffering. Jesus realized this (cf. Mark 14.35-42). The world is not going to be 'saved', in the biblical meaning of the word, by the welfare state or by affluent societies in such countries as Sweden and the USA. Note that although we speak of 'The Suffering Servant', in the EVV of 52.13-53.12 the word 'suffering' is not used. Indeed, 'suffering' is nowhere found in the AV of the OT, either as an adjective or as a noun. The *verb* 'suffer' is found, but only in its original sense 'endure', 'allow', 'permit', as in 'Suffer little children to come unto me' (Luke 18.16).

On 53.11 (pp. 139f.)
In the first edition I wrote: 'The word "a righteous one" (*saddik*) is . . . difficult to construe grammatically, and looks like a distorted repetition of "shall justify" (*yasdik*).' I am no longer sure of this. In Hebrew an adjective almost invariably stands *after* its noun and MY RIGHTEOUS SERVANT would normally be 'my servant the righteous (one)'. But very occasionally an adjective can stand *before* its noun (as here), for emphasis or as a kind of superlative. A good example is Isa. 35.9, where 'the ravenous of beasts' means 'the most ravenous of beasts'. So here the meaning can be 'my (most) righteous servant', which though difficult to construe grammatically is nevertheless not *un*grammatical.